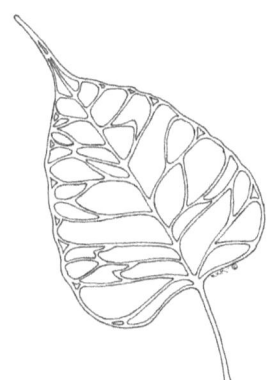

I Am Home!
40 Selected Dharma Talks
For Living Life With Clarity, Love, and Mindfulness

Brother ChiSing (Norman Eng)

I Am Home!
40 Selected Dharma Talks
For Living Life With More Clarity, Love, And Mindfulness

Published by
One Dharma Awakening Heart Dallas Meditation Center

www.AwakeningHeart.org
www.DallasMeditationCenter.com

Paperback 1st edition published September 2018

Copyright © 2018 by One Dharma Awakening Heart
Dallas Meditation Center
Cover and book design by Richard McNeill
Interior artwork by Sakshi Agarwal and Richard McNeill

All rights reserved.

Copyright fuels creativity, encourages diverse voices, promotes free speech, and creates a vibrant culture. Thank you for buying an authorized edition of this book and for complying with copyright laws by not reproducing, scanning, or distributing any part of this book, including images, in any form without express written permission. By upholding copyright laws, you are supporting writers, musicians, and artists.

Library of Congress Catalog Card Number: 2018943915
ISBN: 978-0-69205-76-74

Printed in The USA

Contents

Foreword	i
Introduction	iii
Biography of Brother ChiSing (Norman Eng)	v
Acknowledgments	ix
Brother ChiSing's Letter To The Reader	xi
I Am Home!	1
Bhaishajya Guru: Buddha Of Healing	4
Let It Be	8
All Is Well-Part One	12
All Is Well-Part Two	16
Career Of Enlightenment-On The Eight Fold Path	23
Amitabha: Infinite Light, Love, And Life-Part One	26
Amitabha: Infinite Light, Love, And Life-Part Two	30
Mindfulness: Love Letters From The Universe	34
Quan Yin: Bodhisattva Of Love	39
A Window To The One Heart Of Compassion	44
Simplicity, Surrender, And Surprise	47
A Meditation on Life, Death & Resurrection-Part One	52
A Meditation on Life, Death & Resurrection-Part Two	57
Mindfulness, Buddha, Love, And Emotions	62
The Wandering Mind	66
The Zen Of Messy Enlightenment-Part One	68
The Zen Of Messy Enlightenment-Part Two	72
Be Still And Know	74
Willingness, Willfulness (Dharma Potpourri)	77
Reservoirs Of Positive Energy	84
Universal Awareness-Part One	88
Universal Awareness-Part Two	91
Action And Being-ness	94
Asking The True Questions	98
The Greatest Happiness	103
Buddha, Jesus, And New Earth Spirituality	107
Seeking, Finding, Preserving, Sharing	112
Shortcut To Peace And Happiness	117
Cultivating Mindful Relationships	123
Just Be It	129
Two Aspects Of Our Practice	136
Opening The Door	138
One Divine Nature Manifesting	142
A Buddhist Hanukkah Reflection	149
The Secret Of Meditation	153
The Non-Secret Of Zen	157
Honoring The Clouds Of Our Practice	162

Universal Peace 166
Mindfulness, Monkey Mind, Sangha, and World Transformation 170
Works by Brother ChiSing 174
Music by Cornell Kinderknecht, Co-Director, Awakening Heart, Dallas Meditation Center 175
My Notes 178

Foreword

For over a decade, Brother ChiSing shared his words at our weekly meditation gatherings in Dallas, Texas. He brought a unique perspective and challenged us to be fully present in all aspects of our lives. His talks inspired many over the years, helping countless people encounter life's ups and downs with courage, compassion, and calmness.

One of the appealing qualities of these talks is that the messages are intentionally universal. Although some of the topics and words may come from a Buddhist viewpoint, the concepts and practices are applicable regardless of what faith tradition anyone comes from, including those who are not part of any faith-based tradition. Brother ChiSing often reminds us that meditation and mindfulness are powerful tools that should be open and available for everyone. He also reminds us that meditation and mindfulness are things that we practice. We practice them not because we are good at them, but because they can be beneficial to us. And, like anything we practice over and over, the more we do it, the more skilled we can become. Brother ChiSing would sometimes tell us that he was our cheerleader, nudging us along, telling us, "You can do it!" He encouraged each of us to be cheerleaders for each other, helping everyone along the path of peace and freedom.

Awakening Heart (Community of Mindful Living) and Dallas Meditation Center were founded on the concept that mindfulness and meditation should be available and accessible for anyone who is looking. Sharing and inclusiveness permeate Brother ChiSing's messages. By making his talks available, Brother ChiSing wanted to spread that welcoming spirit of Awakening Heart and Dallas Meditation Center beyond any physical doors or beyond any place in time.

It is our hope for those who read this book that they will see a bit of themselves, feel supported and know that they are not alone.

—Bobbie Perkins, Cornell Kinderknecht
    Co-directors
    Awakening Heart, Dallas Meditation Center

Introduction

For several years, Brother ChiSing had talked of converting his talks into the written word and published in book form. In 2014, Brother ChiSing was diagnosed with cancer, and he requested help in making this dream a reality. A few sangha members and supporters of the Dallas Meditation Center volunteered to collaborate, and came together to begin the work. Sadly, he passed away in 2016, and did not live long enough to see the finished books that continue to bring his voice and message to a wider audience. Two companion books were begun: 108 Reflections published in 2017, and I Am Home published in 2018.

Out of the several hundred recorded Dharma talks by Brother ChiSing, these forty were selected for their power and relevance to enrich and deepen the connections between fellow humans and all life on our planet. The central challenge has been to stay true to his voice and his words. Many hours, weeks, and months were spent going over the transcripts, editing and re-editing, and returning to the actual recordings time and again to stay true to his words. To the best of our ability, while still applying the filter of the editing process, we wanted to allow his light and spirit to shine through.

Our hope is that the written words will dance on the page in a similar way Brother ChiSing energetically presented his talks to groups worldwide. He used his humanity, his own personal day to day living experiences—his troubles, foibles, humor, weaknesses and strengths—from which to draw spiritual conclusions and as teaching tools for dharma lessons.

To Brother ChiSing, the integration of art, literature, and music was important to spiritual growth and to one's practice of mindfulness and well-being. Taking his cue, we developed original art to enhance the reading experience and communicate the playful, creative nature of Brother ChiSing. May these 40 talks speak to you that "just right" message at that "just right" time in order for you to realize pure joy and enlightenment through the words of our beloved Brother ChiSing.

—Valerie Grimes and Patricia H. McNeill, Editors

Biography of Brother ChiSing (Norman Eng)

Brother ChiSing, M.Div., M.A. (Norman Eng) was an interfaith spiritual retreat facilitator, spiritual director, ritual artist, musician, composer, and the founder of numerous meditation groups around the United States. His life journey culminated in an interfaith spirituality, combining beliefs and rituals from both Buddhist practice and Christian faith backgrounds. His ultimate vision was to bring mindfulness and meditation practice to people of all faith and non-faith backgrounds in an Earth-based way, with an emphasis on creativity, music, and the arts. This vision came to fruition as Awakening Heart, Dallas Meditation Center, and One Dharma in Dallas, Texas.

He was born and raised in Texas, lived in California for ten years, and returned to Dallas, Texas for the last ten years of his life. On the morning of March 8, 2016, after living with nasopharyngeal carcinoma for two and a half years, Brother ChiSing peacefully passed from this physical life in his sleep at the home of his family.

His life was a deep and diverse spiritual journey, leaving him with an ever-present appreciation and love of interfaith spirituality. His expedition began with a solid Biblical upbringing in the Southern Baptist tradition, and he received a Bachelor of Arts degree in Religion from a Protestant university. He then journeyed on to complete a Master of Arts degree in Spirituality from a Catholic college. The spirit then led him to a Unitarian Universalist seminary, where he completed a Master of Divinity degree. In 1995, he was commissioned into ministry by a congregation of the United Church of Christ (UCC). During this era, he established several large mindfulness practice groups. He also served as a Youth Director, Children's Director, and Religious Education Director at various churches.

Interfaith spirituality urged him forward to learn more about meditation and mindfulness. Brother ChiSing's primary meditation teacher was the Venerable Thich Nhat Hanh. In 2003, he was ordained by Thich Nhat Hanh with the spiritual name of "True Wonderful Happiness" into the "Order of Interbeing" (Unified Buddhist Church).

The inspiration he received from the practice of Buddhism enriched his Christian faith and strengthened his commitment to interfaith spirituality. Brother ChiSing returned home to Texas where he founded multiple meditation groups inspired by the teachings of Thich Nhat Hanh. These groups came together in 2006 as Awakening Heart (Community of Mindful Living). By 2010, the Dallas Meditation Center was founded with Brother ChiSing serving as the spiritual director. One Dharma Awakening Heart Dallas Meditation Center, a non-profit human services organization, was created in 2014 to provide cost-effective educational programs for the public. These educational programs continue to focus on life-enriching programs ranging from mindfulness, meditation, yoga, qigong, tai chi, as well as health and wellness.

Over Brother ChiSing's short lifetime, his music, vision, heart, and words rippled across the lives of innumerable souls. He filled a variety of roles as he influenced the lives of others.

- Musician:
  Music was a major part of his life. He penned numerous songs and chants. His album, *Buddha Is My Refuge: New Dharma Songs for the Contemporary Sangha*, was released in 2012. Two of his songs appear in the book *Chanting from the Heart* by Thich Nhat Hanh and the Monks and Nuns of Plum Village.
- Leader/teacher:
  He led and spoke at Interfaith, Buddhist, and Christian retreats for communities as small as 10 people to as large as 1,000. He traveled extensively and was a guest speaker at universities, churches, temples, monasteries, sanghas, and meditation centers throughout the United States. He also presented at spiritual and environmental conferences. While in California, Brother ChiSing collaborated on several events and retreats with San Francisco Bay Area spiritual teachers Matthew Fox (*Creation Spirituality, Original Blessing, Techno Cosmic Mass, The Coming of the Cosmic Christ*) and Christian de la Huerta (*Coming Out Spiritually*, Q-Spirit founder and Revolutionary Wisdom co-founder). Brother ChiSing also facilitated meditation groups and retreats in the United Kingdom, France, Hong Kong and South Korea. He also taught World

Religions at the college level.
- Community founder:
  Throughout his short lifetime, he founded numerous groups and communities. While in California, he founded three young adult spiritual/social/discussion groups in San Francisco, Berkeley, and Los Angeles as well as a large meditation community in San Francisco. In Texas, Brother ChiSing founded meditation groups in the Dallas, Houston, and Austin areas. Awakening Heart (Community of Mindful Living), Young Enlightened Souls (YES, young adult meditation group), and Mindful Mondays (mindfulness study group) practice in Dallas, Texas.

It is certainly true that Brother ChiSing accomplished a lot in his short lifetime, and it is important to remember that he was very human. He often struggled with relationships even though he was very well-known and loved. As his illness progressed, he grew more open and receptive to the love and assistance being offered to him, and relationships became less difficult.

Brother ChiSing's book collection was massive. He was a voracious reader, and one of his favorite pastimes was exploring book stores for special gems.

ChiSing loved animated films, Star Wars movies and all kinds of soft, fluffy stuffed animals, which still grace the meditation hall. He bought a life-sized Yoda figure that stood in the meditation hall on occasion and would pop-up in various places throughout the Center; Yoda is still in the meditation hall. Symmetry was very important to him—the meditation mats had to be placed just so, with the cushions plumped, a practice he learned at a strict Zen meditation retreat. He noticed if flyers on the bulletin board were hung straight, and if they were current. And he was not shy about letting the office staff know about any discrepancies. Some, who knew him well, referred to him as a Tasmanian Buddha for his whirlwind approach to life.

Yes, Brother ChiSing was very human, made plenty of mistakes, struggled and suffered, but he will be remembered fondly for his beautiful heart and the light that shines through his words and songs and all those he touched. The communities that he founded continue to create ripples in the present and into the future.

Brother ChiSing's recorded Dharma Talks and the transcripts can be found at: www.AwakeningHeart.org

Acknowledgments

The Awakening Heart, Dallas Meditation Center wishes to express a heart-felt thanks to the group of volunteer collaborators; without their dedication and focus this book would not have happened.

It is a particularly difficult editing challenge to transform recorded talks into consistent readable text. Jessica Hitch transcibed the talks. Valerie Grimes started the book project, selected the 40 talks, and provided the initial editing. The work of completing the editing and the detailed line editing was handed off to Patty (Patricia) McNeill who took the talks to their editing conclusion. Cornell Kinderknecht also provided additional content insight, reviewing each talk after Patty's line edits to help ensure clarity and context and to answer questions that arose during the editing process. He also provided photographs of Brother ChiSing. Rich McNeill was the illustrator, book designer, and formatting editor. Sakshi Agarwal also provided beautiful Madhubani illustrations.

We also wish to thank the beta readers: Bobbie Perkins, Cornell Kinderknecht, Cheryl Muck, Erik Friesen, Kim McNeill, Gaurav Aggarwal, Pam Badger. Thank you, Leila McNeill, for your helpful editing suggestions. Everyone's input was invaluable in completing this quality book.

Thank you!

Brother ChiSing's Letter To The Reader

May 11, 2007

A good student is a wonderful asset to a spiritual community. And what is a good student? Well, I can share with you what a good student is not. A good student is not someone who blindly hangs onto every word that a spiritual teacher says with no room for dialogue. And neither is a good student someone who completely rejects a spiritual teacher or leaves a spiritual community just because of one or two disagreements. In both cases, even though their attitudes are completely opposite, the result is the same: no true learning takes place. Instead, a truly good student is one who opens the heart to receiving spiritual nourishment from the teacher and the community, always checking to see if it truly resonates within and is in accord with general spiritual principles. A good student knows how to dialogue and discern, to doubt and debate when necessary, with an open heart and humble attitude. A good student understands that all teachers are still students, and all students are potential teachers. And, ultimately, there is only one student and one teacher, and no student and no teacher, just vast clear spacious freedom. And We are That.

Affirmation:

I open my heart to learning from my spiritual teachers and spiritual communities. And I affirm the truth of my own wisdom and experience, nurturing the inner teacher within myself. I am both student and teacher and beyond such roles. I am Wisdom incarnate; I am Truth expressing.

I AM HOME!

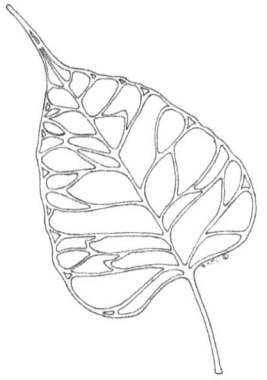

"...and my umbrella turned from this shape...

...to that shape."

I Am Home!

February 10, 2008-Dallas, Texas

A few weeks ago I was scheduled to do a workshop in the San Francisco Bay area in Oakland. Before I left I had a cold and did not feel like flying, so I went reluctantly. When I got there it was rainy and cold, and my ride did not pick me up due to her dead cell phone battery. But I did make it to my friend's place where I was staying.

The next day I asked her to drive me to the BART Station. After she dropped me off, I realized I had forgotten my cell phone. So when I arrived at the station in Oakland, I had no way of calling the person who was to pick me up and bring me to the workshop. The wind was blowing, and it was raining really hard. I was just hoping that somehow they would guess that they needed to pick me up because it was almost time for the workshop to begin. I was sneezing, and I was cold. It was rainy, windy, and dark, and my umbrella turned from this shape to that shape. And in that moment I had to make a choice. But first I want to share with you something that had happened earlier that day that helped me with the choice I had to make.

Since I was conducting a workshop that evening, I decided earlier that day to have a day of mindfulness just for myself. So during breakfast as I was eating my cereal and soy milk mindfully and slowly and enjoying being in my friend's beautiful house, these words welled up from within my heart to my mind: "I am home." And I began to just eat with that phrase in my heart: "I am home"—with every breath, "I am home." I had the realization of the very wonderful deep meanings of that simple phrase: "I am home." And during the whole day wherever I was, I just used that as my mantra. "I am home!"

So while standing outside in the rain, the cold, and the wind at the BART station, in that moment I just started laughing as my umbrella went from this shape to that shape. And I just said, "I am home!" People walking by me probably thought I was a little crazy. But I felt so good because I realized that I had made a choice. I could have said to myself, "I hate this. I don't want this. I am not feeling home right now." But instead I had chosen to tell myself: "I am home to the rain. I am home to the wind. I am home to this weather. I am home in this body, and I am home in this moment."

Then, I checked my pocket and realized I did have my cell phone with me after all. So I called another friend, and he picked me up. We arrived just a few minutes before the workshop started, and I chose to prepare by sitting. Although there were a few logistical things that needed to be done, I decided to prepare my heart by sitting. As a spiritual leader, I had learned that it is important to prepare my heart.

And as I led the workshop for three hours into the evening, I was so full of joy, so full of love. At the end of the evening, every single person in that room shared that they too felt an incredible joy and that their hearts were opened. They really got the message of "I am home." In fact, that was what I had shared with them: "I am Home."

Seeking Home

As we start to practice meditation and spirituality in our lives, most of us are just trying to be at home in the here and now. A few weeks ago someone said, "I am a seeker." A lot of us start out seeking, trying to find that peace. People ask, "Where can I find peace? Where can I find that stillness and that peace inside and around me?" And so in the beginning stages of our practice we are trying to center, we are trying to ground, and we are trying to be at home in the here and now. We are trying to be home with this body and mind, at home with peacefulness.

And eventually we will have a glimpse, perhaps a few small glimpses at first, and then maybe a definitive glimpse, a breakthrough into the deeper meaning of 'I am home'—"I am one with God. I am one with all. I am Buddha nature in expression." And you do not need to look for it anywhere else because everywhere you go, you are there. Everywhere you are, God is, as Christians would say. Everywhere you are, Buddha is. "I Am Home!"

Enlightenment is not just a one-time deal. Enlightenment is who you are, and it breaks through over and over and over again. As my teacher Thich Nhat Hanh says, "Enlightenment never ends." Enlightenment always unfolds, always manifests and expresses infinitely. I remember one little glimpse I had a couple of years ago after a retreat. My friend and I were at the retreat at the same time, and we decided to stay an extra day. And so we woke up in silence, nodded and mimed to each other: *We're going to walk, and then we're going to meditate and sit, and then we're going to go and eat.* We did everything in silence. And then we went to the tearoom, got two cups of water, and sat down with our cups. And I sipped very slowly, very deeply, very mindfully, very gratefully, for fifteen or more minutes—from that one cup.

And suddenly my heart opened up like before; once again it opened and expanded. And I just felt all of the water in that one cup, all the water in my blood, and all the water in the oceans, rivers, and clouds of the earth as one water. And I realized that whenever I pollute the waters of the earth, then I am polluting my own body. And if I pollute my own body, I am polluting my whole planet. Remember this is our home; this is the home for all of us. Maybe not everyone is ready to practice sitting meditation or walking meditation, but I think everyone can practice drinking water meditation. If every single person would drink their water mindfully and share this practice with their friends and schoolmates and coworkers and congregations, then I believe we will have a profound collective breakthrough and awaken to our oneness, to the inter-being of all things, all beings.

We are home! We are love!

Thank you!

Bhaishajya Guru: Buddha Of Healing

July 19, 2015-Dallas, Texas

Visits From The Buddha Of Healing

During one of my hospital stays due to a cancer diagnosis, I asked some ministers to come and be with me, even if just for a few minutes to talk or to pray. You know, one thing I learned is that it can be really lonely in a hospital. So if you know someone who is in the hospital, please be a Medicine Buddha and go visit them. It would really mean a lot to them; I know it would, because it meant a lot to me.

Reverend Michael Gott, a good friend of mine and one of the ministers at the Unity of Houston church, came to visit me. He actually came to visit me on his birthday, so I felt honored that he took the time to come and see me.

He prayed with me in an affirmative, positive way, and he held my hands. Afterwards, he said, "Whoa! I've prayed for many, many people, but this is the first time I actually felt energy in my hands." And I was thinking, "Of course you felt energy."

I had another energy experience during a visit with my acupuncturist, Dr. Alan Chen. I was lying there for an hour with needles in me, trying my best to meditate—breathing in and breathing out, saying a mantra, a prayer—and I started to daydream. That is when I felt a tingle move up from my feet. It literally felt like someone had just touched my leg, and it kind of shocked me. I opened my eyes, and there was no one else in the room. So I took it as a reminder from Medicine Buddha to go back to my practice and not to indulge in all of those random thoughts. Random thoughts are okay, but they will not heal you. So always come back to your mantra.

Another time at the acupuncturist, I saw a beautiful blue light spinning with lots of sparkling filaments very powerfully in my mind. I thought, "Oh it is an octopus!" I humorously called it my healing octopus because in this visualization the light came and all the filaments reached into my head towards the tumor and just began to suck out the cancer cells. I have been trying to use my healing octopus from time to time and allow the healing energy to remove whatever is obstructing my health.

The Medicine Buddha Woke Me Up

Before having lots of health challenges and finding out I had cancer, I woke up suddenly one morning. I do not really know what I was dreaming of right before I woke up, but I had Medicine Buddha in my mind. Even though I knew about Medicine Buddha, I had never really studied in depth about that Buddha; yet I knew I was being asked to learn the Medicine Buddha mantra, and to do it in Sanskrit.

The Dharani Medicine Buddha Mantra:

Om Namo Bhagavate Bhaisajya-guru Vaidūrya-prabha-rājāya Tathāgatāya Arhate Samyak-sam-buddhāya Tadyathā: Om-Bhaisajye Bhaisajye Mahā-bhaisajye-raja Samud-gate Svāhā

On the day I received the impetus to learn more about Medicine Buddha, I went to Barnes and Noble. Looking at all the spines of the books in the Eastern Religion section, I noticed one in an interesting color, so I picked it up. The title of the book was *Letting Go of the Person You Used to Be* by Lama Surya Das. I opened the book randomly. And guess what chapter I opened to? Medicine Buddha! In that moment I knew for sure that Medicine Buddha was calling on me to learn this practice. I believe that Medicine Buddha was preparing me for the healing journey that I was about to embark on, not only for my sake, but also for the sake of others.

It took about a week or two for me to memorize it. It was difficult as there was not really a melody for it that I knew; so I just modified a melody for it based on Tibetan chanting with my own style. There is beautiful power in this dharani, and I tried to make it easy for you to memorize by putting a tune to it. It is my own non-literal spiritual interpretation. (You can listen to it at **www.AwakeningHeart.org**.)

I affirm the principal reality of enlightenment, healing, spirituality, and all the inherent qualities of my Buddha nature as fully embodied in awakened teachers and awakening beings. Therefore, I also affirm the practical realization of enlightenment, healing, spirituality, and all the qualities of Buddha nature—physical, mental, emotional, environmental, and relational, and so forth—in myself and in all beings here and now.

Your Personal Healing Practice

I want to share five healing practices that can be helpful in your life, at least on the physical level:

1. Reduce sugar, dairy, and heavy meat intake: If you are not a vegetarian or vegan, that is fine, but try to reduce the amount of heavy meat you consume. And if you are going to have some meat, choose to have organic; it makes a big difference.

And sugar, refined white sugar, is just not good for you. It is actually a toxin, and even some of the big-money companies are starting to confess that they are purposely putting sugar in almost everything to get you addicted to their products.

I suppose a little dairy is not going to hurt you, but if you are drinking three glasses of milk every day, you might want to reconsider. Statistically, countries that have the most dairy consumption also have the highest levels of cancer. I do not really know what the correlation is yet, but it has a lot to do with inflammation. Certain foods like sugar, dairy, and meat cause your body to become inflamed. If your body has too much inflammation, it becomes harder and harder for the body to heal itself. So just try to reduce your intake of foods and drinks that are inflammatory to your system.

2. Increase your drinking of pure water: Your body needs water; water is so important for flushing out toxins in your body. A lot of us are very dehydrated, and we need water to get the lymphatic system working properly. Also, make sure it is purified water and not tap water. Depending upon where you live, these days it can be harmful to your health to drink tap water; some cities and states are worse than others.

3. Check your Vitamin D3 level: Are you deficient in vitamin D3? If you take a multivitamin, and it says vitamin D and not D3, then you might want to reconsider switching to another brand, because it is important to have vitamin D3. The body does not really process Vitamin D; it treats it like a foreign element, but vitamin D3 is much more biocompatible. You can also get vitamin D3 by being out in the sun, but how many of us are going to be out in the Texas sun on a hot summer day long enough to get the amount of vitamin D3 that we need?

4. Have an 'earthing' practice to really be in touch with the earth. You know, our modern lifestyle does not really encourage us to be in touch with the earth anymore. Be in nature and walk barefoot on the grass; hug a tree, and hike in the mountains, or whatever. It is important to be in touch with the earth, because the earth has an electromagnetic field that is very healing for us. And even though it is blocked by buildings and roads, it is fine, because as you know, those buildings are a part of who we are as humans. But let us also be in touch with the earth again.

5. And then last but not least, exercise. Even if it is just walking 15 minutes in the morning and 15 minutes at night, it is better than nothing. Walking is very, very good exercise. If you can, practice yoga or qigong or anything that gets you moving. Sometime in your life you could become so ill that you might not be able move around very much; and if you did not have a regular lifestyle of healthy or even minimal exercise, it will be harder to get through. So, if your body is conditioned, it will be easier to get through that period.

These are five practices just on the physical level. Do them on your own as you reflect on your life and on your practice.

Let It Be

April 5, 2009-Dallas, Texas

Let it be. That is our practice. There is really no need to talk. Let it be.

Today is Palm Sunday, the beginning of holy week for Christians leading up to Easter Sunday, the Sunday of new life and Resurrection. So as the Buddha is not only a teacher for Buddhists, I also believe that Jesus is not only a teacher for Christians.

They and other teachers of the world are universal teachers. Mother Mary is not just for Christians either; she comes in many forms and has many names. In the Buddhist tradition, we may call her Quan Yin, the Mother of Compassion. She is that part in each of us that is able to 'let it be,' able to include and embrace anything, able to open the heart of love and light for all beings.

This morning as I sat in meditation at my parent's house, I heard the door open and could hear the little footsteps of my sleepy three-year-old niece. I guess her father, my brother, was not yet awake. So, she walked into my room, saw me meditating, and laid her head down on my lap, and she slept there for 20 minutes.

I poured forth 'metta', loving-kindness meditation from my heart—wishing her well, wishing her happiness, and enjoying her presence. And in that moment I was embodying Quan Yin or Mother Mary. Then after 20 minutes, she got up, left, and walked out the door as if nothing happened. I continued to meditate for another 20 minutes. She had left the door open, so I could hear my family in the kitchen. I decided to just send metta loving-kindness to them all, wishing them wellness and happiness. For the next 20 minutes, it was relatively quiet, and I sat there in that gratitude, in that love, deeply receiving that spacious light.

Pure Potentiality

The first spiritual law of success according to Deepak Chopra is the law of pure potentiality, the true nature within us all. It is that true nature within us and all beings that is the source of everything, the source of our wisdom, the source of our creativity, the source of understanding insight, and the source of compassion and love. Mother Mary and Quan Yin both represent that deep, universal compassion. It is beyond any name, expressed in many ways by many names.

When we meditate, we get in touch with 'being-ness.' The law of pure potentiality refers to being-ness as the ground of being. I remember being in walking meditation with a friend a few weeks ago outside the monastery, and we shared from our inner center, from our 'knowing-ness.' My friend calls it that 'knowing.' I kind of like that word—*knowing*. I never called it that before, but it is true; it is that which knows. It is the 'knowing'. And so we just channeled words from that center, from that 'knowing' to each other. And I shared words of wisdom with her, and she shared words of wisdom with me; it was very beautiful, very wise, and very powerful. It truly came from that place of pure potentiality, our true nature—'that knowing,' 'that being-ness.' Every day we can live our lives from that place of pure potentiality. We do not need to struggle or stress about our next step. What should we do? Where should we work? Where should we live? Who should we be with? We do not have to stress and struggle about that because there is already that center within us that is the knowing—the pure potentiality that is the being-ness, the wisdom and compassion. Simply let go of that which obstructs you from realizing it. Simply be.

Let It Go

When we sit, we are not struggling and doing. And if you are struggling a lot when you are sitting, then perhaps you should look at it a different way. Sitting meditation is not like going to the gym. Sitting meditation is about letting go—it is just a matter of being and getting in touch with who we already are. And so as we sit, we just relax. We rest. We release. We let go, and we are with our 'being-ness' here and now.

It is a little bit hard at first because a part of us identifies with other things besides 'being-ness'—other things like 'thinking-ness' or 'making lists-ness' or 'planning-ness' or past 'memory-ness.' It is like a busy bee or a monkey mind. But, in fact, that is not really who we are. That is just the part of us that we overly identify with.

As you practice your daily meditation, formal sitting, and living in mindfulness throughout the day, you start to realize that although the busy bee is still flying around or that monkey mind is still jumping from tree to tree, there is another reality that has been there the whole time: I am breathing; oh, I've been breathing the whole time. "Oh, there's this body living this whole time, and there is this inner knowing the whole time."

There has been an inner awareness the whole time. And it is not like you were the monkey mind and now you are the Buddha mind. No. That spacious quality of 'being-ness' and awareness has always been there, just as your breathing has always been there all along with these thoughts and ideas and whatever else. Our practice does not help to get rid of all of that, but identifies with it and helps us to re-identify with our pure potentiality, our pure 'being-ness.' And as we do that, naturally the thinking and the busy bee mind will slow down and will start to focus and cooperate. Instead of being our enemy, it becomes our friend. We never eradicate that part of our mind; we are simply showing who the boss really is. The 'inner knowing' is the true master. And when the mind serves that, then ego and personality and whatever else is no longer a problem. Mind is now a channel of expression for that Buddha nature in the world.

I will close with a poem* that came to me after a seven-day retreat:

> Turn around and look within.
>
> Can you see the sound of silence?
>
> Can you hear the flowers smiling?
>
> Can you taste the setting sun?
>
> Do you know that I am the one?
>
> Do you know the one is you?
>
> No separation, no birth, no death.
>
> Only this moment, only this breath.
>
> No self to suffer, no gain, no loss.
>
> All is perfection, even the dross.
>
> Do you know that I'm the one?

Do you know the one is you?
Namaste.

* This poem was turned into a song "Do You Know" on Brother ChiSing's CD: *"Buddha Is My Refuge"*, song #7

All Is Well-Part One

July 19, 2009-Dallas, Texas

During walking meditation tonight, I noticed that we are all walking at our own pace, in our own way, with our own different bodies, and at our own different rates, speeds, and shapes. And I realized we are just like the subatomic particles that are doing the same thing, just like the planets and the moons in the solar system, and just like the suns and stars in the galaxies. This is our reality when we practice, even if it is just glimpses here and there.

I also thought about how some of us, as we practice in silence, say to ourselves things like: "Amitabha," "All is well," "I am home," or "Here and now"; while still others are just feeling and not even thinking anything. Yet we are all able to practice together through the universal language of silence. And silence can be the expression of our unity and diversity, so all of our beautiful diversities can come together and practice together in the silence of our unity.

And thinking about our unity, I expand that to our connections with others in the world, particularly those who are practicing in a similar tradition as ours like the Bat Nha community in Vietnam of 400 monks and nuns. Just a couple of years ago, Thich Nhat Hanh, our teacher, was allowed to go back to Vietnam for the first time after several decades in exile. The government finally allowed him to go back, and one of the monasteries where he used to practice opened its doors to him. And the monks said, "Please come and enjoy practicing here, and bring in your monks and nuns to teach others your ways." So for the last couple of years they had been doing that, but this past week local governments and some of the local Buddhists have started to oppose Thich Nhat Hanh's community. They cut off the water supply and electricity, basically trying to starve out the monks and nuns.

We have brothers and sisters all over the world, including in Vietnam, who practice under difficult conditions. So as you practice, do not just focus on yourself but practice knowing that you are practicing in solidarity with others. And I hope that you will practice this coming week in solidarity with the monks and nuns at Bat Nha in

Vietnam, sending your 'metta,' your loving-kindness, and your mindfulness, so that they will do well in the practice.

The Sneaky Universe

But even if they get thrown out, it is not the end of the world. Sometimes difficult situations occur because it is the sneaky universe's way of spreading the Dharma. I mean, think about the Dalai Lama and Tibet. Of course it was a terrible thing when the Chinese government took over Tibet, but because of that the Dalai Lama and many Tibetans fled; within just a few decades they had spread the beautiful jewels of this secret kind of Buddhism from Tibet all around to the rest of the world.

And when Vietnam exiled Thich Nhat Hanh, which too was a terrible thing, it resulted in this practice that we are practicing here and all around the world which help hundreds of thousands of Westerners to relate to the practices of mindfulness in a way that is relevant for us all. And so I believe that the results of the persecution of this community in Vietnam are such that, although they were thrown out of the monastery, I believe that it could be the sneaky universe helping the Dharma spread across Vietnam and Asia in this particular way.

In Vietnam and in many other Asian countries, Buddhism had become somewhat ritualized and was only about meditation and chanting, not about meditation and practical modern ways of practice. That is the reason why so many people love the way of Thich Nhat Hanh and other teachers, because they are presenting the practices in a more relevant, modern way. And so I see these monks and nuns going out to other monasteries, practicing and helping to spread a kind of practice that is more relevant, a practice that is more socially engaged and practical. And maybe that will transform Vietnam in the next few decades and spread across other Asian countries, and you may see most of these practices transform all of Asia by the next century. You just never know.

All Is Well

So this goes back to the mantra that came to me in meditation a few days ago: "All is well." Even if there are difficulties or negativities or changes of circumstances in our own personal lives, in the midst of it all and at the deepest level, there is the truth of 'all is well.' These mantras that come to me once every six months to a year are extremely powerful. They are not just like a passing thought, but they are as if my innermost wisdom speaks very loudly and clearly to me. In the past there has been:

"Here and now"

"I am home"

"Thy will be done"

To me, they all mean the same thing as 'Amitabha,' the Infinite Light. All of them are the same meaning, just expressed in different ways. I share that with you to encourage you that no matter what—*all is well*. There is something greater at work in the universe, and you might not be able to see the full picture from your perspective, but when you are in touch with your true nature deep within, there wells up that encouraging energy that says 'all is well!' So we can continue to practice, even in the midst of difficulties, even if our mind is going crazy, even if our body is aching, and even if we are feeling fidgety, for 'all is well'. And even if monks and nuns are being thrown out the monastery, all is well.

Monkey Mind In Action

I am reminded of a Chinese proverb:

> There was a farmer who had an older son who was helping him in the fields. One day one of their horses ran away, so they had less help on the farm; and all the neighbors said, "What bad luck." And then the next day the horse came back with another horse, and then all the neighbors said, "Ah, what good luck." And as the son was trying to tame this new horse, he fell off and broke his leg, and all the neighbors said, "Ah, what bad luck." Then the Chinese army came through and enlisted all of the men of a certain age into the army and took them away. Most of them would probably never see home again, but they did not take the farmer's son because he had a broken leg, and all the neighbors said,

"What good luck."

And so this reminds me of limited thinking—the monkey mind, the ego mind, the judging mind that simply tries to label things as good luck or bad luck. But at the deepest level of true Buddha nature, true wisdom, there is only everything just as it is, and all is well. Now I used to really not like it when people would say, "Everything is perfect," "All is well," or "It's all good," or even, "That was just meant to happen." I hated that; I just thought it was so superficial, hokey-pokey and New Age-y until I had my eye opening experience, a glimpse of enlightenment, just a small line: 'Oh, all is well!'

But that truth is already within each of us, and whether we have had an opening tonight or not, each of us will have many openings, more and more and bigger and bigger. It is just never-ending. But even if we have not yet had a first glimpse, that truth still resonates at some deep level of our being. And so when we practice, we can even taste it. You know? In each breath, in each step, in each heartbeat, in each molecular vibration, all is well!

All Is Well-Part Two

July 19, 2009-Dallas, Texas

Editor's Note:
This particular dharma talk was in a Q and A format and captures the playful wisdom of Brother ChiSing. We are leaving it in the original format, lightly edited for clarity, and some of the audience member's questions have been condensed to present just the question, rather than to include any personal references.

Brother ChiSing:

I would like you to ask questions and let them come from your heart, and let us see if there are any answers that come through me.

Audience Member:

"There is one part of Karma that I do not understand. You see some people who do bad things, and they have what seems to be a good life, and then you see some people who are very good people that seem to have bad things come to them. And I understand that they have built up so much merit from previous lifetimes and that merit is still playing out in this lifetime. It has to come to pass."

"But I wonder, what if life is a spiral, an evolution? Then don't you get better each lifetime? I mean, would these people be doing bad things to the environment and other people, and yet bad things don't happen to them because they have good merit stored? Isn't life an evolution where you get better each time?

Brother ChiSing:

In our practice, we try not to guess someone's past or our own past. We try not to worry too much about our future or someone else's future, but we practice with being here and now because the present contains the past and all the seeds of the future. So if we can just work with our present karma, our present situation, then that is enough. We don't have to worry about past or future. Also, it is almost impossible for the small human ego mind to understand these things. And it is an endless loop in the mind to try to wrap our head around it.

So a better way of approaching it is that on one level it may be true that some people's fruition of their actions occur immediately, or it is delayed. We see that in nature. Sometimes a plant doesn't always come to fruition right away. So, on one level, that is true; on one level karma is being played out. But at a deeper level, all is well. At a deeper level, whatever is happening, whatever someone else is doing to you is happening for you; at a deeper level, it all works out.

And you can't say, "Oh, that poor person! They are born into a deformed body. They are in a poor country, and it is because of the bad things in their past lives." I don't think we can really say that because we don't know if it is not because they're actually a highly enlightened being coming into the world in a condition to teach someone else about compassion. And actually at the deepest level of reality, all of us are highly enlightened beings who come to play roles that help each other to learn certain lessons.

So, I guess on one level, there's the good karma and the bad karma, and it is just working itself out. But at a deeper level, we are all Buddha. We are all divine nature, and we are just willingly at some deeper level allowing ourselves to come into manifestation to help each other, to learn about wisdom and compassion, to express the infinite. So really at the deepest level, we don't need to worry about karma. At the deepest level, all is well.

Audience Member:
"What is karma?"

Brother ChiSing:
Karma literally means action. But in this sense, it can mean two things: action and the fruit of action—so the cause and consequence. So usually when we say karma, you might either be talking about someone's action or you might be talking about the results of their action coming back at them. We learn from the good experiences, and we learn from the negative experiences. As long as we are learning, then it is still a positive thing.

Audience Member:
"When it comes to all is well, sometimes I find it easy to be in that reality, to be more unified with that truth. Sometimes I find it very difficult to be unified with that truth."

Brother ChiSing:

Well, there's all is well, and then there is **all is well.** We can say the words in our minds or with our mouth, but we are not really expressing the deepest manifestation of that truth except as we continue to practice and let go and be with reality just as it is deeply. Then there comes a point when you don't have to say all is well. Something deeper is saying **all is well**, and you simply flow with that. So, in the Buddhist teachings, there is this teaching of two truths, and that is why it is sometimes confusing depending on whether the teacher is speaking from one type of truth or the other.

One truth is called relative truth, and the other kind of truth is called absolute truth, although I don't like the word absolute. But one is the kind of truth that you deal with in just everyday life, right? Yes, some things are good, some things are bad, some things are high, some things are low, some things seem ugly, and some things seem beautiful. You're just working with the relative world of comparisons. So when a teacher speaks to truth in those realms, they might say: "This is good. This is bad. Don't do this, do that." And that is because they're working with people who are only at the level of understanding that kind of truth.

But then at a deeper level there is the other kind of truth, which is 'ultimate truth'; I like that better than absolute. You know, there is the truth of: "Yes, you know killing is not so good, and giving and helping the poor is good. Right? Bad and good." But then at the ultimate level, it is all good. 'All is well' because everything plays its part to create Buddhas. Without some kind of difficulties and sufferings, we don't really grow. We don't really have wisdom or compassion without these kinds of circumstances, so this is actually the perfect kind of environment to mold baby Buddhas into mature Buddhas.

Whenever you hear teaching, just ask yourself, "Is that teacher speaking at the level of relative truth or ultimate truth?" Because sometimes, they will sound like they contradict each other. Karma is only a teaching on the level of relative truth. At the level of ultimate truth, there is no karma. There is no karma; but they are not opposed to each other. The ultimate truth is expressed in the relative truth, and the relative truth is an expression of ultimate truth. So even in the midst of the karma, there is that depth of no karma. And even in the infinite reality of no karma, it is always being expressed as karma. So just be mindful when you hear a teaching. Are they speaking at relative level of truth or ultimate level of truth? They are not opposed; they're just two perspectives.

Audience Member:
"I rarely ever get attached to anything really negative. I just let it go and so rarely get angry. But at the same time, I feel like maybe detachment from the whole anger thing is healthy for me anyway. However, if things are really happy and joyous, I also don't attach and get really invested in that either. What is going on?"

Brother ChiSing:
In an ultimate level, there is this being. But at the relative level, there's this human body and mind learning about emotions. And in a way, it is okay that we have this range of emotions. In a way, we are evolving the capacity to express through emotions. Yes, when things evolve, we kind of experiment; we kind of overdo certain things. But that is all part of the experimentation of the evolutionary process. So from the larger perspective, it is all good because you're learning as you make all kinds of goof-ups and mistakes, right? So on the relative level there are mistakes, but on the ultimate level there are no mistakes, because they're all helping us learn as a whole.

But as far as on a relative, practical level, I would talk to this emotion thing. We have emotions, and in our practice, there is also the aspect of us that is simply being-ness and awareness. So part of our practice is to be able to give space to these human emotions in a safe space—awareness and being. And eventually, when we give it that safe, gentle container, they actually start to transform. We don't have to do too much to them; we just allow them to transform.

Every feeling has the right to be heard. The flipside of the truth is that no feeling has the right to control your life. So every feeling has the right to be heard, because there is a message underneath every emotion, no matter how negative you label that emotion, like anger or depression or whatever. There is a deep message there, something to learn from. So our practice is to make a safe enough container so that the deeper message can be heard deeply in our very being.

And of course, as we hear the message, automatically the emotion then shifts and changes. Why? Because no emotion is just an emotion. Like there is no such thing as solid anger or solid sadness; it is just energy. Sometimes the energy molds itself to something that feels like anger, and then it changes and molds itself into something that feels more like sadness or molds itself and feels something like peaceful joy or something else. It's all just energy.

And this points to the truth of emptiness. In other words, nothing is a discrete, solid entity. It is empty of that because it can change to something else. Because actually, everything is simply energy, and even at a deeper level, that energy is simply consciousness or mind manifesting as energy, manifesting as matter, et cetera, et cetera… So, nothing is solid.

That is why the Buddha taught about 'non-self.' There is no solid self; it is so much more flexible and spacious. That is true of you, and it is true of me, and it is true of everything in the universe. The whole universe is simply a play of energy and consciousness so that we have the privilege of learning and evolving from baby Buddhas to mature Buddhas. That is why from the ultimate perspective 'all is well' because everything is here for our growth and learning—everything! And that is why with the word "all," it takes practice to actually get it. We can say, "All is well, all is well, all is well," but that doesn't really mean anything. Only when that deep place opens, then you really see the "all." The whole picture is well, despite the particulars of it which are not quite positive and not quite well, and which don't feel very good. Yeah, in the world of the relative, all is not well.

Audience Member:
"Brother ChiSing, I am learning and experiencing more well-being. For example, when facing issues my practice is helping me. How does that work in a love relationship when two people are on different paths? Do you have anything to share about that kind of energy exchange that happens between people?"

Brother ChiSing:
That is one of the other geniuses of this practice. It helps us to

be with the changing and the malleable, flexible nature of everything, including relationships. It is only when we hold on to something and try to make it solid that we suffer even more. Obviously, there is this normal everyday reality where there is pain and difficult feelings, but we add onto that our own mental pain, mental suffering on top of just the normal pain that happens in life. It is because we have in our minds: "Oh, I'm supposed to have my one and only prince or princess charming, and they're supposed to look like this; and it is supposed to be like this, and it will last this many years." We have these concepts, and whether they are conscious or unconscious, we have them. And whether they come from our own individual thinking or the collective thinking, they are there. When we do our practice, we deal with them. We have to practice with 'well, it is not so solid' and 'it is not really that way.' You know?

I know married people who are miserable, and I know single people who are very happy. I know single people who are miserable, and I know married people who are happy. It is not about whether you are single or in a relationship. It is about whatever life is presenting to you at this moment. Are you able to work with it? And if you have the belief that 'I'm supposed to have this,' well, guess what is going to happen?

And that is why it is a practice for most of us, because the practice is just like the sutra we read a few weeks ago, "This is the Greatest Happiness." Can we be happy in this moment as a single person? Can we be happy in this moment as a married person or a person in whatever sort of relationship? Can we just allow someone else to be their flexible, malleable changeable nature and allow ourselves the same?

One thing I learned about relationships came from my father. I used to actually look down on my father because he was very materially oriented, always working very hard, making money. And he wasn't that interested in spirituality other than just doing his dues by going to church once a week. But a few years ago, that all shifted when I realized the truth of 'inter-being,' and at least on one level I realized it. Because my father was the way he was, making money and working very hard for the family, I didn't have to worry so much about working hard and making money. I could take classes in things like religion and philosophy and other "useless things," as my mom puts it, and I could go to retreats often. Because he was the way he was, I can be the way I am; there is not a separation at all. So really, I can only be talking in front of you and practicing with you because of my father.

So before understanding 'inter-being,' I judged, and I criticized; and I saw things separately—like that was good and that was bad. But after understanding a little bit of 'inter-being,' I realized: "No, he can be who he is because that allows me to be who I am." So even though you may be looking for a partner who is perfect or who practices the same meditation style as you or has the same taste in movies or whatever, just let that all go because maybe your perfect partner is just whoever is right there in front of you along with whatever it is you're learning from them and growing through with them. That is wonderful!

And partner doesn't just mean romantic. It can be friends and teachers, all kinds of people. We have many, many partners. We are simply being together in all these different partnerships to help each other learn the true meaning of 'all is well.' And we are creating that moment-to-moment: "All is well!"

And even in relative truth where all is not well, we are working to create the kingdom of heaven on Earth, the Pure Land of the Buddha on Earth until that day when we can all say of all races, all colors, all orientations, all religions, all cultures, all languages—
All is well.

Career Of Enlightenment-On The Eight Fold Path
March 1, 2007-Dallas, Texas

I would like to start off with reading something from my journal writing practice. A couple of years ago as some of you know, after my sitting meditation I began to write in the morning, whatever came to me from the deepest part of me as if it was the Buddha in me speaking to me. So this following reading is about right livelihood:

Right Livelihood

Right Livelihood is one of the spokes of the noble Eightfold Path of liberation. In the traditional enumeration it is number five, and yet, in fact, it is like the eighth—this is the culminating point of your practice, of right view, right intention, right speech, right action, right effort, right mindfulness, and right concentration.

You are a Buddha, and you are here to embody and manifest the truth of who you are in this universe of form. Your right livelihood is an expression of your right purpose and right mission in this world. Your career is the career of a bodhisattva, an awakening being. Your work is the work of embodying and manifesting your Buddha nature, your true self, right here and right now, in this realm of time and space and energy consciousness. How you sustain your physical life is intimately connected with how you sustain all of life.

The whole Eightfold Path is contained in right livelihood. It is your job to bring right view and right intention into your work, to bring right speech and right action into your career, to bring right effort, right mindfulness, and right concentration into your livelihood. This is your job behind your job.

Your true work is to be here now and to bring your true presence into daily life. Your true work is to bring loving-kindness into the world, to radiate peace in places of disharmony, and to be the wisdom that you are, applied to all walks of life. Whatever you do to sustain yourself, your family, and your world—whether it is farming, teaching, nursing or whatever profession—remember your true profession: "You Are a Buddha!" This world is your workplace, and you are here to embody and manifest your true nature in an infinite variety of ways: through art, music, and poetry; through religion, education, and politics; through sexuality, culinary cuisine, and architecture; through community building, ecology, and medicine; and through all the ways you work to sustain yourself and all of life.

Be the Buddha That You Are

Be the Buddha that you are. It is time now, my sisters and brothers, my dharma friends. It is time now to remember who we are and to allow our lives to reflect that knowing. We are not simply here for the reason we think we are. Our true career is the career of awakening, the career of love and kindness, the career of wisdom and understanding, the career of bodhisattvas and Buddhas. It is time here and now, moment to moment, to breathe, to smile, to sit and to walk, to speak and to listen, as the Buddha that we are. It is time to radiate and share from a generous heart of abundance—a knowing and a remembering with all beings. Because all of us—no one excluded—*all of us* are the Buddha.

You do not have to become a minister, or a priest, or a monk to live the life of your Buddha-hood, the career of enlightenment. In the very midst of being a mother or father, a teacher, a worker, a garbage man, a flautist—whatever your profession—you can be the Buddha in that place. Do your work with love and mindfulness; serve all beings by serving one being; love all beings by loving one or two beings; embrace all beings by embracing three or four or five beings, here and now.

Just Do It

You do not have to struggle and strain to do it.

"Just do it!"

Right effort is not about creating more suffering and pain in your life; right effort is the effort of effortlessness. It is to commit yourself, to make your vows, to live the life that you are meant to live in the spirit of graciousness and grace, in the spirit of knowing the abundant support of the universe, in the spirit that Thich Nhat

Hanh calls "busilessness" and that the Taoists call "effortlessness" or effortless effort.

You *do* do it.

You do create mindful action, but it is not the small separate ego self that is doing it. When we are relaxed into our vastness, our true nature, then it is the whole universe working through us, as us.

So, in that spirit, dear friends,

just do it.

Amitabha: Infinite Light, Love, And Life-Part One
June 21, 2015-Dallas, Texas

Editor's Note: This talk covers cosmic Buddha and Bodhisattva archetypes. It is good to have some background in basic Buddhism, so if needed you might want to study a little bit on the basic teachings of Buddha. The Four Noble Truths and the Eight-Fold Path will help you better understand the other levels of dharma. Suggested reading: The Heart of the Buddha's Teaching by Thich Nhat Hanh.

Infinite Light And Infinite Life Buddhas

In the mythological interpretation of Amitabha-Infinite Light, there is a Buddha in a cosmic realm called the Pure Land. The name of this particular Buddha's Pure Land is Sukhavati; *Sukha* means happiness, and *vati* is a loving place of happiness.

But there is also another Buddha named Amitayus meaning Infinite Life. Sometimes in the presentation of these Buddhas, they can be thought of as two different Buddhas. Most practitioners over the centuries and especially now consider them to be two aspects of the same Buddha—a more popular name is Amitabha, but you can also use Amitayus.

A few years ago I realized that the combined infinite light, infinite wisdom, and infinite life of your existence implies infinite love because the light of wisdom and the light of service to all beings is of course centered in infinite love.

So you can think of Amitabha as not only meaning infinite light, but also infinite love and infinite life. The dharma is said to be like an ocean, where the very edge of the beach is shallow, and even little children can splash there and play. Or you can go a little bit deeper and even deeper, for the ocean is very vast and quite deep; the dharma is like the ocean.

There are many levels to understanding and interpreting dharma. When some people interpret Amitabha Buddha, there is a mythological reality of Amitabha. There is also a universal collective reality, a here and now reality that I call the unfolding reality, a future reality, cosmic reality; and well, I added this one: *ultimate reality*. I have no idea what that one means because I have to be enlightened first, but I will put it there. This is really my way of outlining and looking at different interpretations of Amitabha. You will not find this in any textbook; it is just my understanding through practice.

The mythological reality of Amitabha Buddha and the reason why Mahayana Buddhism arose in the first place is basic Buddhism, and then 500 years later there arose the development of another level of interpretation of Buddhism, of dharma.

Brother ChiSing SIDE BAR:

Shakyamuni Buddha, Quan Yin, Amitabha, Medicine Buddha—all these Buddhas and Bodhisattvas can be seen as separate beings. Or like me, you can also see them as just different qualities and manifestations of the one Buddha nature, one true nature.

The Great Vehicle

The next level of interpretation is called Mahayana, meaning Great Vehicle. And it is Mahayana Buddhism that started to become more popular around the first century of this era.

Since you have both a right brain and left brain, part of you likes to think scientifically or logically with your left brain. In fact, Buddhism was one of the very first spiritual traditions to be more scientifically oriented. Sometimes it is hard to respond to scientific, logical, and mathematical kinds of formulas; so you cannot ignore the right brain. The right brain responds better to dreams, visions, poetry and stories—basically mythology. But mythology can also sometimes point to something real.

Mythology is simply a way of creating a story to help people experience that reality. Whether or not that story is literally true is not the point. The point is to practice with that story so that it opens up certain depths of the subconscious mind in your right brain and all these other deeper levels of your being beyond just the left brain, your logical mind. It helps you to manifest and experience the reality through the story.

The Bliss Of Nothingness

There were stories that developed around Amitabha during the first century. One was of a practitioner many eons ago in some other realm who was a servant of Buddha. He wanted to understand about the function of the Buddha. In other words, what does one do when one becomes a fully enlightened Buddha? Well, in early Buddhism, there was this attitude that when a Buddha finished the work in the physical realm, each Buddha just enjoyed being in a state of bliss forever. In that way, one would think of Nirvana as a sort of extinction into the bliss of nothingness.

But as practitioners kept practicing over these few centuries of time, they started to have other understandings and interpretations of what it means to be Buddha, and so for them, the emphasis was on what the Buddha does. Every Buddha, according to Mahayana Buddhism, creates a Pure Land; it automatically radiates from their being. So wherever there is a Buddha, there is also a Pure Land. Pure Land or Buddha-kshetra means Buddha field or field of enlightenment—a field of positive energy of wisdom and compassion and skillfulness to help serve all beings.

So, in this story Dharmakara made 48 vows. He made these different vows saying how he wanted to create a Pure Land where all beings could benefit from his practice and his energy, so that they would also become enlightened.

The Buddha that he was attending to basically helped him have what might be called an astral projection, and his spirit was able to visit all the different Buddha lands, all the different Pure Lands in the universe to check them out and to see how each Buddha made their Pure Land so wonderful and beautiful and attractive to all beings.

A Pure Land Model

Dharmakara then decided he was going to make a Pure Land based on all the other Pure Lands. His Pure Land would have even more beauty and be even more attractive, and his Pure Land would be the easiest to access.

The reason this is one of the most popular stories in early Mahayana Buddhism is because this story is a template, if you will, to understanding our practice. The ideal here is the bodhisattva, a being on the path of enlightenment to full Buddha-hood, who develops vows and practices and skillful means along the way. So by the time the bodhisattva is a fully enlightened Buddha, each bodhisattva will have all of these amazing ways to help people of varying mindsets.

I like this story because it is a reminder that our practice is not just for our own sake. As we practice mindfulness and meditation, it is not just for our own bliss and peace. This is an inspiring story for our right brain, reminding us of our bodhisattva intentions and that the greater reality of our practice is cosmic and is to be interconnected with others.

Amitabha: Infinite Light, Love, And Life-Part Two
June 21, 2015-Dallas, Texas

Amitabha: Our Own True Nature Now

Amitabha is the universal reality of life and love that is as infinite as existence itself. Different religious traditions call it different names, but it is this universal reality that is the source of our every breath. But not only is it universal, it is very personal *right here and now.* So Amitabha is referring to that light and love and mindfulness right here and now in your own true nature.

So, not only is the true nature of light and love and life here and now in you and in the great potential of who you are, it is also the love and light that keeps unfolding in your life. You know, it is like saying: "Yes you are all manifestations of Buddha nature!" But is that it? Is that the end of the story? No! You have to think about Buddha nature and let it manifest. So that is the unfolding reality of allowing wisdom and compassion and willfulness to permeate your life. It is not meant to be just a potential seed within you. It is meant to grow through you and through us all.

And it is not only your personal wisdom and compassion that are growing. You and others are building something collective. We are all here to create the Pure Land on Earth. And so your vision, the Mahayana vision, is to remind you that it is not just about the afterlife, even though mythologically it is part of the story. Here is the funny part: even though many people want to be reborn in the Pure Land when they die, it is a bit different. In this story if you go to the Pure Land, you get to become a Buddha and continue practicing; . And what do you do when you become a Buddha in the Pure Land? You do not stay there; you always come back or go to different realms to serve and help other beings.

Can I Sit On My Butt In Heaven?

So the story of the Pure Land is different from the story of the afterlife in heaven. In this story, it is maneuvered in such a way as to not let you just sit on your butt. It is like a little Buddha push to remind you that enlightenment is not just about personal awakening, but about a collective awakening that reflects the future. We cannot destroy Planet Earth by mindless actions, forgetting our children and grandchildren and their children and the future generations. That is not true with the dharma.

True dharma must have that vision of the future in mind to create the Pure Land on Earth, as well as the Pure Land everywhere. And then that will lead us to the cosmic understanding. It is not just the Pure Land on Earth, but in every realm in every world, in all the universes, this is the great movement of dharma. Not only is it for our planet and our species, but it is for all planets and species, all realms of existence.

And as you become fully awakened Buddhas in the universe, what will happen once you are enlightened? I have no idea, but I think it is going to be awesome! I think that this is our ultimate destination—full Buddha-hood, not only as individual Buddhas, but as collective Buddhas.

That is what I think of when I think of Amitabha. I do believe that there could have been a man called Amitabha. More than that, I believe that Amitabha is a word referring to a collective reality. I like to use the word Amitabha to refer to my Buddha nature, to the collective love and wisdom of all Buddhas and bodhisattvas condensed into one word. Amitabha evokes in my heart a remembering of the support, the Pure Land support that I have.

Adding Light In The Pure Land

So as I am practicing mindfulness, I am walking in the Pure Land of the Buddhas and Bodhisattvas of Amitabha. I am walking in their light; I am walking in the energy of their practice. And of course, this is not just about Buddhas, but also the bodhisattvas throughout history, including our spiritual teachers that are alive today, like Thich Nhat Hanh. I consider him a major bodhisattva because he makes it easier for me to practice. He brings the dharma to me in a way that is relevant and practical. And so whenever I experience peace and love and joy, I am walking in a Pure Land, in that Buddha field that they have all contributed to over the centuries.

I think of the Pure Land as a collective reality. It is almost like every single time someone practices mindfulness, it adds a little ray of light into the Pure Land. Then as we all practice, we are actually contributing energy to the Pure Land and not just receiving the energy of the Pure Land. In each mindful moment, we shine a ray of light into the Pure Land, so the Pure Land keeps growing as a manifest reality on Earth.

To me, that is what the word sangha means. Sangha is the Pure Land—communities of mindfulness. Of course there is also the Pure Land after you die, but a more important interpretation while you are here on Earth before you die is the Pure Land here and now.

Depending on where you are in your life journey, you may need both teachings. If it is early in your life journey, you really need to focus on the Pure Land of the here and now on Earth. But of course, for those who are in the process of transitioning into the afterlife, it is very, very, very comforting and helpful to focus on the Pure Land of the hereafter. That is the reality here and the reality there; they are not separate, but one.

Deep Peace, A Gift Of Experience

A few years ago, I was practicing just breathing in and out with Amitabha, just feeling my breath and feeling my heart filled with the Infinite Light of the Buddhas and bodhisattvas. All of a sudden, I felt as if a wind or a breeze from the Pure Land wafted all over me, through every muscle; and not just physical muscles felt this breeze, but also my mental muscles. Everything relaxed into a deep peace.

In my internal and deeper aspect of myself, I knew what this was. I had glimpsed the reality of Amitabha and the Pure Land, because as I sat there, I realized, "Oh, everything is a gift! The past, present, and future is a gift. Existence is a gift; enlightenment is a gift." Even though I have to practice and open myself up to allow it to manifest, it is this self that is also a gift.

And when I breathe in and breathe out mindfully, where does this breath come from? That is also a gift. And when I sit here so comfortable on these nice, modern cushions, where do these mats and cushions come from? Yes, they also are a gift.

And the motivation to practice meditation, mindfulness, spirituality, and enlightenment—where did those come from? Not from my ego! It comes from the universe as a gift; it comes from a collective gift of reality. It comes from all of the spiritual teachers who kept the practice going no matter what. It is because of them I can practice. Because of others, I can practice. Because of the trees giving oxygen, I can practice. Because of the sun shining its light, I can practice and be alive.

In that moment of realization, just for a few minutes, I can feel pure bliss and trust. Before that, there was always this little edge of worry: "Am I doing it right? Am I doing enough? How long is it going to take before I get enlightened?" But at least in those few minutes of practice, all of that just melts away, because I realize that everything is a gift.

So my practice is just simply to sit in it and to allow it to flow through me and manifest. It means that everything I do or do not do stems from a place of deep knowing that I am always embraced, that I am always supported. My enlightenment is guaranteed so nothing is going to be able to stop that. Nothing is able to stop the wisdom and the compassion that flows to me from so many beings, from so many Buddhas and bodhisattvas.

In the Christian tradition, there is a verse in one of the letters from Paul that reads: "Nothing can separate me from the love of God—not persecution, famine, government powers, spiritual entities." None of that—no circumstances can separate you from the reality of wisdom, compassion, and spiritual power that is within and around you.

Amitabha.

Mindfulness: Love Letters From The Universe

October 25, 2015-Dallas, Texas

I have just returned from a trip to Minneapolis where I had been a scheduled speaker and led meditations for a group of students. I almost did not go and had canceled several times before because I was nervous about speaking in front of a large group. I was also a little bit scared as it is sometimes difficult to fly when having health challenges. But I decided to just do it slowly and mindfully, to not overdo it, and to ask for assistance.

A Shift In Perspective

One thing that helped me to travel and get over the nervousness of speaking to a large group was knowing that I would be sharing the dharma with all of these wonderful college students and adults, and I was going to spend time with my peers, my friends, and my Zen teachers, rejoicing in our good work.

That perspective helped me relax and look forward to sharing the dharma with eager students and to also have a sweet time with my friends. I am very grateful to the enlightened ones and all of my angelic helpers who took away my fear of flying and gave me the energy so that I could get there and share.

In the audience were college students from three different universities, and after the meditations and teachings, they were so full of bliss, hope, and encouragement. I could see that many of them seemed inspired to practice more diligently in their lives and to create a whole new generation of mindful practitioners. I also had a couple of practice sessions with peers and adults, and those were very sweet. I was able to go into deeper teachings with them and really share from my heart.

Distraction And Mindfulness Practice

One of the students asked a question about out-of-body experiences and other dimensions and realms, and whether or not it was okay to use substances to help you have these experiences. My answer was: "Who you really are is an infinite, eternal being. You have already explored many realms and will explore many more realms, and when you leave this human body-mind construct, you will be at one with the infinite once again in a very conscious way. So as a human being, you don't need to worry about all of that."

I then suggested to her: "Put your focus more on being here in the present, on being a human being. You don't need to worry about other realms; you don't need to worry about past lives; you don't need to worry about the afterlife. Where you want to focus is on this life. So instead of trying to get an out-of-body experience, try to have an in-the-body experience through mindfulness, rather than escaping and distracting."

The number one addiction in America is distraction, in my opinion. We seem to always want to distract ourselves from being fully present here and now. The real point of life is to actually be here, to really taste the food we eat, to really see the flowers, to really hear the music, to really feel the wind caressing our face and the sun warming our body—to really be present.

Love Letters From The Universe

There is a lot of religious talk about worshiping God with praises, songs, words and prayers, but I think the best way we can praise God is to actually appreciate what God has made here. The best gift that we can give to the creator is to appreciate the creation; that is the way we say thank you. Every time we feel our breath with gratitude for life, every time we mindfully eat our food with appreciation and truly taste each bite, every time we mindfully hug our beloved ones, and every time we take a step on the earth with full presence, that is our thank you to the universe. That is the real true praise and worship.

Many years ago during a meditation, a metaphor came to mind. There are many, many love letters from the universe, from the divine, from our true nature all around us. There are love letters everywhere, also inside of us. But they are in an envelope that is sealed and can only be opened through mindfulness. Every time we are mindful, we open up a letter and really see and appreciate and receive the contents of the letter. So when practicing mindfulness through meditation or chanting and being fully present in activities throughout the day, we are opening up reality and receiving this beautiful message from the universe.

I think it gladdens the heart of the Infinite when we receive the letter—when we receive the message. Imagine how you would feel if you wrote a beautiful letter to your beloved, and they said, "Thank you," but never opened it? It gladdens the heart of the Infinite when we not only praise the envelope, but actually open the envelope and read the letter and receive the message. Through mindfulness and meditation, we start to realize that the flowers and the grass and the trees and the people and our lives and all of the experiences that we are having are all sending beautiful messages to us, important messages to us, one of which is the most fundamental message of all—that *we are loved.*

We are addicted to distractions which can manifest into mental and emotional problems affecting many areas of our lives, especially our relationships. I believe the fundamental core issue is that we do not realize how much we are loved by God, which is why we do not seem to love ourselves. When we do not know that we are so deeply loved, it is very difficult to love ourselves. When we do not love ourselves, it makes it very difficult to really love others.

The spiritual practice of mindfulness, through meditation in daily life and being fully present, is the number one way to open that love letter from the universe and really receive that message that indeed transforms your life and the lives of everyone that you touch.

None of us really know when we are actually going to end our time here. So start a mindful practice now. Read your love letters from the universe, and remember to inspire others.

Make Ripples

There are many budding bodhisattvas that hear my talks and read my teachings, and my wish is to inspire them so that they will continue to do the work even after I have left this body. I love that idea. The positive ripple effect of our lives is so powerful.

And I am so grateful for each and every budding bodhisattva because when I look at them, I do not see just one person, I see many,

many beings. I see many, many ripples because the ripple effect of each person touches hundreds of people. So in fact, if we look at those around us through dharma eyes, we will realize there are thousands of people there or even more, millions perhaps. Our lives are not just our individual lives; our lives are always a ripple of effects on all others around us. So let us make sure through mindfulness that it is a positive ripple effect and not a negative ripple effect. There are enough negative ripple effects throughout history, so let us now change history.

I believe the 21st century will see the greatest shift in human consciousness. The ripple effect of our positive mindfulness will transform the present and the future and heal all that we have brought from the past. Remember to read those love letters!

Quan Yin
Sculpture circa 900AD
Beijing, China
Photo 2011
Courtesy Richard McNeill

Quan Yin: Bodhisattva Of Love

July 12, 2015-Dallas, Texas

Editor's Note: Avalokiteshvara (Sanskrit) originated as a male figure in Indian Buddhism and is represented in different cultures as male or female. In China, Avalokiteshvara is represented in the female form as Quan Yin. Interestingly, there are also images that appear ambiguous, embodying both the male and female form, as in the Quan Yin photo on the left.

I am noticing in my own personal life that Quan Yin (Avalokiteshvara), the Bodhisattva of Compassion, is more important to me now than ever before. In most artistic renditions of Quan Yin, she has a headdress, and in the top part of the headdress, there is always the image of Amitabha Buddha, the Buddha of Infinite Light, Infinite Love, and Infinite Life.

To me, all of these different cosmic Buddhas and Bodhisattvas are both symbolic and real at the same time. I think human mental concepts and understandings cannot fully grasp these cosmic realities with language. But we are humans, and we have language; so we have to use human language to talk about these things.

What I mean when saying they are symbolic is, that at least on the earth, there was never a historical person named Amitabha Buddha; and perhaps there was not even a historical person named Quan Yin or Avalokiteshvara. So in that sense, they symbolize the qualities of love and compassion which are our true nature and which manifest in these symbolic forms.

However, at the same time, I also consider them real because the energy that they represent—the love, the compassion, the light—is real. Whenever someone on Earth embodies the qualities of this kind of love and compassion and light, then they become a channel of that Buddha energy, that bodhisattva energy. Every time we chant the name of "Amitabha" or chant "Om Mani Padme Hum," which is the main mantra of Avalokiteshvara, we evoke these same qualities through our practice. I believe we are getting in touch with the energy field that many others in the past have helped to create.

Creating the Buddha Field

I believe an infinite life and love and light already exists as the basis of our reality and holds everything with compassion. So that is real. When a person on Earth awakens to those qualities and fully embodies those qualities in their life, they become like an icon giving us a glimpse of that infinite reality through a human being, and then they start to create this energy field. In Buddhism we call it Buddha-kshetra, which is known as Pure Land; but really, it literally means Buddha field, a field of Buddha nature, a field of Buddha enlightenment, a field of Buddha wisdom and compassion. They start to emit and radiate and begin affecting others, a whole community and then many more communities, and a movement begins that eventually affects the rest of the world.

Whether practicing, chanting, meditating, or whatever, we attune to this energy of compassion and add to that energy field. Throughout the centuries, every single practice has added to that energy, and now in the twenty-first century, we are the heirs of all the love and compassion that has ever been practiced throughout space and time. And is it not wonderful that we also add to that energy for future generations? So we receive and give simultaneously whenever we chant, whenever we meditate.

I believe that Quan Yin has manifested many, many times on Earth through many different human beings, whether full-time for their whole life or just part-time. Sometimes we are not fully enlightened, but there are moments in our lives when we are fully in touch with that true heart of compassion and wisdom and have a thought, a word, or an action that is truly an expression of Quan Yin or of Buddha. To me these are all just different human symbolic representations of this one true nature, one Buddha nature, with many different ways of expressing those qualities.

Quan Yin is the energy of Amitabha Buddha. But because of the limitations of our human language, we might not immediately understand the story. According to the story, Amitabha Buddha is supposed to stay in his Pure Land, in his realm of beauty and bliss, teaching all of these beings—many, many beings—to become enlightened; he has a pretty big job.

But how does he take care of all these people here on Earth? It would be impossible by the way the story was told to say, "Well, Amitabha comes down to Earth," which he cannot, because of our human limitations on the story. Well guess what? Avalokiteshvara, Amitabha's assistant, comes down from the cosmic realms to the Earth and appears through humans or through whatever form you need. I know Native Americans have spirit guides who are animal guides, and I believe that can also be an expression of Avalokiteshvara appearing as an animal. But Avalokiteshvara will appear in any way you need and might even appear as a good friend when you really need a listening ear. Can you see how that works?

Quan Yin Manifested on Earth

Over the centuries, many stories have been cultivated and developed into various incarnations of Avalokiteshvara. Especially in China, women seem to really embody the qualities of Quan Yin, this Bodhisattva of Love. Whether or not these stories are literal does not really matter because their purpose is to help us notice her and recognize her and realize how pervasive she is in our lives, and that she should not be taken for granted.

I have done a lot of the more masculine energy work in doing my best to keep up with my spiritual practice and to figure out which modalities are best for my healing from cancer and other things; I am exhausted from all of that. Sometimes, I just want to give up because this is so much work, and this is the reason why Avalokiteshvara and Quan Yin are so important to me these days. Quan Yin and her motherly, compassionate, and gentle energy just wraps me and reminds me that it is okay. We do not have to do it all; let the universe help. We do not have to do it all by ourselves.

I love Quan Yin's energy. It is just another way of reminding myself that there is that motherly, compassionate, heart energy available to me; and when I feel like giving up or I feel afraid, I can call upon my divine mother. So at the end of our meditation, when we are given the option to pray silently, I just visualize Quan Yin as a motherly figure putting her hand on dying patients, putting her hand on soldiers, and putting her hand on all kinds of people all over the world.

So, Quan Yin is an extension of this Amitabha Buddha energy of light and love and life that represents our infinite Buddha nature, which is who we really are and what the universe is really all about. As human beings we have temporary amnesia and delusions about things, and that is okay; the Buddha totally understands.

We might think the Buddha is some sort of grandfatherly figure who will beat us until we become enlightened, and that might be a carryover from some religious stories from our upbringing. But that is not true; there is only love and compassion. Sometimes a Buddha or bodhisattva might have to manifest a little bit of tough love energy when necessary. That is true, as I have had my fill of those as well; but honestly at the end of the day, even if tough love has to manifest for our benefit, we can still rest in the loving embrace of compassion.

Try Dharma, Not Drama.

I have a friend who has been going through so many different changes recently. It is kind of overwhelming, and I totally get that. And so I said, "Let's pull a card from my spiritual deck and see if our angels or guides or bodhisattvas—whatever you want to call them—might give us a little helpful hint on what to do with all of this drama that is going on." And so we pulled a card that said: "Please get over yourself." I love that! That is like a tough love moment with compassion and gentleness. It was not a harsh demand, but soft and loving as in: "Oh, honey, get over yourself."

One day I'm going to make a bumper sticker that says: "Try Dharma, Not Drama." Because we can really drown in our own dramas, we need to remember to try dharma, not drama. We all have things happening in our lives at different times, some more intense than others. But if we do not choose dharma in those situations, we will easily, easily fall into the trap of being drowned in the drama. So that is why we have to choose dharma and keep practicing in every moment. One of the things that helped me to get through some of this stuff a few months ago was to keep up my gratitude practice. If the only things that I say to myself and to others is only all about that which is not going right in my life … *blah, blah, blah*, then that is what will fill my whole consciousness, and I will only feel worse. That is why we have to turn it around with simple practices like gratitude: "I am grateful."

For example, right now, I am blind in my right eye from the tumor, and because it has been so long, the doctor thinks that the optic nerve is damaged long-term. I am not going to say permanent, because nothing is permanent. Right? And I am starting to have some dimness in my left eye, and that scares me. I do not know what is causing it, and I do not know if it is going to get worse or not. But instead of focusing on: *Oh, my God, I'm going to be blind and so on*; I ask myself: *Ok, well what do I know right now? I don't know anything about tomorrow, but what I do know right now is that I can see.* Even in limitation, I can see green and red and blue and beige and pink, and I can see candles. I'm just so grateful that right now in this moment, I can see. Even though I cannot read any of the small print books I have, I have found ones with larger print and am so glad I can read those.

The more I do that, the less overwhelmed I get by the drama. I believe that gratitude is really the primary practice of those who follow the teachings of Amitabha and Quan Yin. It is all about shifting our perspective and remembering. The practice of chanting the name of a Buddha or bodhisattva over and over and over again in Sanskrit is called *buddhaanusmrti*, which means "mindfulness of Buddha" or in other words, "remember what is true."

That is what gratitude does; it allows us to see more. When we are not practicing gratitude regularly, no matter what good things may come our way, we will not even see them. And it is a part of our mindfulness practice to really see. So mindfulness and gratitude are not separate; just as Zen and Theravada emphasize meditation and mindful living and chanting and gratitude like the Pure Land teaches. They are not different, and they are not separate. They are different forms of practices, but they are not separate; mindfulness and gratitude go together. That is why I think prayer and meditation go together too. All kinds of practices go together, that is why we have both walking and sitting meditations. They balance each other out.

A Window To The One Heart Of Compassion
February 21, 2010-Dallas, Texas, Lunar New Year

Many years ago when I was in college, I had a roommate named Juan, and he told me about something that had happened to him when he was a teenager. He was in a car accident just outside of his house, and as he began to bleed and lose consciousness, he felt his spirit leave his body.

He began to float above his body toward this beautiful light; it was so peaceful, so beautiful, so accepting, and he knew he would be safe if he went toward the light. And so he headed towards the light, into this infinite love, this vast acceptance. But then he heard his mother screaming, "Mijo! Mijo!" She was crying and praying to God, "Please don't let my son die!"

And in that moment, he knew that it was actually his choice in that particular situation. He could continue on to the light, which would be wonderful, or he could go back out of compassion for his mother and for all the work that he was meant to do in his life. Obviously, he made the choice to come back since he was my roommate several years later.

I have never forgotten that story. Since then, I have heard similar stories from friends and other people who have confided to me their personal experiences. So even though I have not had that kind of an experience myself, I have absolute faith that those experiences are real. There is no reason why my friends would lie to me, and so I trust them.

I also trust these experiences because I have had unique experiences confirming to me the reality of a spiritual universe where we are not this separate self, this 'body-mind'; we are the vastness itself which cannot be described in words. Yet the 'body-mind' does not always recognize that, and that is okay. But through the practice of mindfulness and meditation and spirituality, there is a waking up that happens, a deep knowing that happens.

Is It Just About Transcendence?

For many of us we think that the spiritual journey is about transcendence, and that is actually a very important part of the journey to go from lower levels of reality to higher levels of reality. That is definitely part of the journey, but that is not at all the totality nor even the goal of the journey.

I think that my friend's experience really embodies the ultimate goal of what the journey really is, if you want even to call it a goal. It is not to go away from here, and it is not to leave behind the mundane physical realities in exchange for a higher plane of existence, even though that is part of the journey. Rather, it is waking up to the light that we are, waking up to the fact that we already are that transcendence. What is there to transcend? We do not really need to transcend; we are already that beautiful transcendence. And when we wake up to who we really are, we will remember why we are here in the first place.

Some spiritual teachings tell us that this body is evil; this earth is fallen, and we are all sinners by birth. Can you imagine that? Tell me any mother who would look at her baby and say that this child is a sinner. It is ridiculous, and only man could have come up with these kinds of ideas.

There are people who think that this world is terrible and evil, and it's just a bad idea that God made me. No! I do not believe that! We are here for a reason, and we too can awaken just like my friend Juan. He had an awakening experience in the very moment he was transcending to the light, and the truth in his heart was deep and powerful. If we can wake up to who we are and get in touch with truth in our hearts, we too will remember why we want to be here.

I know that it can be a struggle and difficult; there is a lot of suffering in this world. I struggle; we all have our struggles and suffering. There are days when I really wish I could just go on to another life. This world just seems like so much trouble. But when I wake up to the truth in my heart, that truth in my heart says: "No. Be here now; remember why you came to this earth in the first place.... Be that light that you are in the darkness, be that hope in places of despair...Or be like my friend Juan, to be there for his mother." He would have been fine transcending toward the light, and eventually his mother would have been fine. But he chose to come back because he remembered in his heart why he was here in the first place.

Seek Peace, Seek Remembrance

So in your practice, do not seek bliss; seek peace instead. Do not seek eternal pleasure; seek eternal service and helpfulness. I know it is difficult, and I am not saying that you should not have joy in practice. You definitely need that for encouragement. But if it is the only reason why you are practicing, then you are missing a big piece of the puzzle. Come back to your heart. This is why Jesus came, because no matter how much he suffered, He did it because of His love. And this is why Buddha came, because no matter how hard the trials, he wanted to become enlightened for the sake of *all* beings.

You are here as a Christ, as a Buddha, as a divine being. Do not forget who you really are just because of the human disguise you have. There is a purpose for your human disguise, a reason for your particular parents and your particular upbringing. It is so that you that can serve your particular world in your particular way, with your own particular gifts.

I know it is hard as human beings, and that is why we meditate, to remember and then come back fully here and now. Meditation is not about transcending everything; meditation is about remembering. Meditation is remembering who you are and finding encouragement to really be here, here on the earth, to let "... thy kingdom come, thy will be done, on earth as it is in heaven."

That is what the Pure land of Amitabha Buddha symbolizes. In our meditation we get in touch with our reality in the spiritual realm which allows us to then bring it down to Earth—the Pure Land here and now, the beauty here and now, and the light here and now. And through our words, through our actions, through our relationships, and through our unique gifts we are each a portal of the one divine heart. Each heart is actually a window to the one heart that shines in all the universe.

Simplicity, Surrender, And Surprise

May 6, 2007-Dallas, Texas

Recently, when I was in Minnesota leading some workshops and retreats, I had the privilege of working with Reverend Carolyn from one of the United Church of Christ congregations in Minneapolis. I really love the UCC denomination there; they are very openhearted and open-minded.

She invited me to lead a retreat at her church which had also opened its doors to another church. On Sunday after church, I was invited to give the sermon in a worship service. It was a musical service and very creative, a really wonderful experience. I was working with the youth group as well, and I had them do walking meditation with me outside. They all said that it was "cool."

Reverend Carolyn was also responsible for opening the doors for me at United Theological Seminary near Minneapolis to lead their chapel. It was wonderful to speak to seminary students who are training to become ministers. I believe it is so important for our spiritual leaders to understand the importance of mindfulness and the effective power of meditation practice—the contemplative dimension of our spirituality—not just theological practice, liturgical music practice, or social justice practice.

Very rarely do I find ministers that come and want to help, actually staying for the whole day-long retreat. Many times, in my experience, they like to plan, help, and do other things, but then when it comes to actually joining in with the whole day of meditation retreat, they will just say hello and then goodbye; they do not stay for long. And I am not sure why that is. Perhaps they feel that it is not needed because they have already been trained in seminary. But I can guarantee you that I went to seminary myself, and they do not teach you this kind of spiritual practice. But Reverend Carolyn stayed and loved it; she wanted to stay, and I loved seeing her there.

On the last day, she and her husband drove me to the airport. She told me of a dream she had that morning. In the dream I handed her a pair of glasses; they were her glasses, but I was handing them to her. And they were shiny and bright, with new lenses in the glass frame. She said it was an extremely spiritual, powerful dream for her. And I immediately knew what the dream meant when she told me, and it was very humbling. Basically she was telling me that this dream symbolized her own experience of practicing the whole day at the mindfulness retreat, meditating together with others and with me, and bringing a whole new light to her spiritual practice and journey.

It was not that I had given her anything that was not already hers. Anytime a spiritual facilitator guides you, it is not that he or she is giving you anything that is not already yours, maybe they just put a different spin on things, providing new lenses so you can see more clearly. Maybe the lens that you have is discolored or covered up with dirt and dust. The facilitator simply helps to clean them and make them look brand new. So when we put them on we can see clearly the truth of who we already are, the truth that has always been ours.

I love her dream. It is so perfect. As a facilitator we give each other what is already ours, and with cleaner lenses we can see more clearly.

Simplicity, Surrender, Surprise

At the mindfulness retreat, I gave a short talk about our practice being a practice of returning to spirit. There are three qualities of returning to spirit: simplicity, surrender, and surprise.

Simplicity

My first Soto Zen retreat was very strict, a very strict format and a rigorous schedule with a lot of sitting meditation and very little else. And it was not very meditative for me, even during eating meditation. We had to eat really fast using the chopsticks and the bowl in a certain way. And if you are not finished, you do not get seconds; they just come around, and if you are not finished, they go on to the next person.

Eventually, I kind of got the hang of the whole routine because there is a reason why they adhere to this routine. It is to help you be really mindful of the order of things, all of the details; Japanese Zen is very into details.

And I remember every day, we would sit on the same cushion and the same mat, and then we would have to get up, bow to our cushion and mat, and then brush it and fluff the zafu.

Yet the thing is, it was extremely clean in that room, because everyone was so, so clean. And after three or four days of this, I just kept thinking, "It's clean already!" But I did not say that out loud; I just breathed in and breathed out, and I just did as I was told.

I do not really know what it is about the fourth or fifth day of retreats, but on the fourth day of a retreat, something happens to me during that period of time—maybe it just gives me enough time. The first day I really enjoy it. The second day it is starting to get a little hard. The third day I am miserable. By the fourth day I have a breakthrough. On the fifth day I just love it there. And that is just my pattern. I do not know what it would be for others.

Surrender

On the fourth day of the Soto Zen retreat, the bell rang, and we got up to bow to our mat and cushion. Then, as I hit the mat it was as if my hand was the universe, sweeping the universe, and every moment of the motion was completely present. *And I got it!* In that very moment, I got it—at least in that aspect of the practice, I got it! I felt tears in my eyes; I just felt such joy, and realized one purpose of this act. I realized that this very act is a practice, for if I can truly take care of these dust particles, if I can truly love the mat with all my being, then that is the foundation of loving others. It is what I realize every day we vow to save all beings in the Zen tradition: "Countless beings we vow to save, ceaseless afflictions we vow to end, limitless dharma doors we vow to open, the deepest path of awakening we vow to realize." It is the foundation of loving yourself, loving your neighbor, loving other creatures, loving the world, and loving the universe.

So how can we possibly save the whole world, liberate other beings, or love other creatures if we cannot even bring our whole being into loving this simple moment, right here, right now?

And Now For The...

Surprise!

I remember on my very first retreat with Thich Nat Hanh, I made a good friend named Elizabeth. She invited me to come visit her in Nashville, Tennessee, and we had a wonderful time as we rode bicycles and walked around the lake. She showed me the forest path and many other things. It was so beautiful there.

She let me borrow her brother's bicycle, and as we biked down a trail we went into a residential section to get to the lake. While we were there the wind started to blow a little harder, and suddenly I felt my hat starting to blow off from my head. So I just kind of reacted and tried to grab the hat, and as I grabbed it I realized that I was not really a great cyclist. And so my next thought was that I had better put my hands back on the bike and let go of the hat. And so I did, but what I did not realize until a second later was that I had put my hands on the handlebars with both the front and back brakes pressed.

And then time stopped; I began to fly, and it was just wondrous—the sky, the clouds—and the sky and the clouds and—*oh, the blacktop!* I hit my chin first; then my hands reacted, and I scraped my palms down as I tried to break as much of the fall as possible. But then my bike turned too and fell on top of me just to add things to that experience.

Well, I did not really have any words to say at that time, and actually I could not have because the wind was knocked out of me. But my friend Elizabeth was just screaming as she turned me over and saw the blood. And when she saw that I was still alive, she was just so happy.

I actually felt sorry for her because I knew, just based on what I was feeling, that I was really okay for the most part. I was really feeling bad for her because I was thinking, "I must look awful. My hair must be a mess right now." And so as I was feeling sorry for her, I tried to comfort her and reassure her that I was not dead and was okay; nothing seemed to be broken. I just needed to relax in that moment. And as we were on a hot, asphalt road, I spotted an oak tree, and I asked her to please just gently roll me to the grassy area under the oak tree. And she rolled me over gently because it was too painful to be dragged, and I just sat there.

And it was so nice to feel Mother Earth under my back and to look up at the sky through the leaves and the branches of the tree. In that moment there was nothing to say, nothing to do—just be with the grass under my back, just be with the sky and the tree, be with my breath which was so precious at that time. I just felt so much gratitude and love for that tree as an expression of the divine, as an expression of Buddha nature, of everything taking care of me in that moment.

If it had not been for my bike accident, I would never have noticed the beauty of that oak tree. So sometimes the universe sends things our way to help us stop and pay attention to our lives and our surroundings.

But we do not need to have accidents or emotional incidents for this to occur. That is why we practice mindfulness every day and every week with each other, so we can be accident prone without the accidents. Our practice of mindfulness makes us accident prone, prone to the accidental grace of the universe, to the truth, the goodness and the beauty available always.

We are not the clouds of our emotional dramas and thoughts and ideas and stories. We are the vast sky and spaciousness of the here and now.

A Meditation on Life, Death & Resurrection-Part One
April 20, 2014-Dallas, Texas

There is sickness and health, caterpillars and butterflies, life and death, and there is here and now. During a recent 10-day Healing Qigong Retreat where many had come together for an insightful experience, I had my own personal moment of insight and self-awareness. I had seen in my mind the image of a caterpillar changing and creating a cocoon around itself, and then transforming into a butterfly. I realized that this was a message from spirit to me as this is exactly like what I am now experiencing on my healing journey with cancer. Although several possible meanings had come to me, it did not matter which meaning was correct, for it was still a caterpillar changing into a cocoon and becoming a butterfly. Either way, it is a wonderful, wonderful, and beautiful thing.

From Caterpillar to Butterfly

In one scenario, I am leaving behind my old self at the midlife point and going into the cocoon where I am resting, taking care of myself, and putting myself into a healing environment—a healing process. What is interesting is that as I am healing through cancer, I am also realizing that this physical disease is an opportunity for me to find the deepest meaning in my life. How do I reconcile with the past? How can I live fully in the present, open to co-creating whatever future is possible?

Another scenario is that if I live through this healing journey, I know that I am going to be a very different person than who I was in the past. My ministry is going to shine 100 times brighter, and my sincerity and integrity will be even more intense, more true and honest. I am already feeling that. I have healed through so much unforgiveness, resentment, bitterness, and regret already. It is amazing how I have been able to let go of so much already in this healing journey, and I know there is more to come. And I feel, even though my body has been going through things physically, my spirit and Qi field are shining more and more every day. It is an amazing thing.

And if I am to die physically, I will still become that butterfly released of all that has been holding me back and letting go of all resentments and regrets. I will find the jewel of the meaning of my life and move on into a realm of love and light and life eternal. I know that already. I know that if I die, what awaits me is so wonderful; there is no reason to be afraid. I will probably laugh at the moment I leave my body. There is so much human fear around death; yet it is so small of a thing compared to the grandness of what is ahead. So when I think of that. I realize I *get* to become a butterfly. I *get* to release the shackles of limitation. I *get* to be free once again, and that is wonderful! And that realization takes away the fear of death for me.

One More Possibility

The cocoon may be something that is a process through which I will live 40 or more years sharing the light, and in that sense, I will be a butterfly too—I will be a new person, a new being. And all the wonderful things I have learned about health and wholeness and healing has been amazing! I know truth at a deeper level than ever before. And it is an interesting experience because I had known something in my mind, but now I know it in my heart; I am beginning to really know it in my gut. It is very amazing when that happens.

With any of these possibilities, the butterfly is a guaranteed scenario. So there is nothing to really worry about; I love it. Whether we live or die, it is great, and it is amazing. Wow! Really think about that; whether we live or die, it is amazing! It is awesome. *Oh, hallelujah*!

Struggling in Sickness?

In our sharing circle at the Healing Qigong Retreat, a man shared that he did not feel like he knew where his home was—just never felt at home with himself. He had been searching all his life for a feeling of being home, and he had never found it. The message from spirit came for him and for the whole group, and I heard these words in my heart of hearts; I hope you hear them too. "Home is who you are when you are no longer looking elsewhere."

A woman was sharing about how hard it was to hold her hands up for the 30-minute movement practice without dropping her arms. Part of the practice was to keep them up and be mindful of the breath and the movement. However, on the third or fourth day of this difficult practice, a memory from her childhood suddenly came to her. She was in the ocean on a flotation device with her arms up on the device. She had been trying to learn how to swim, but now she was just floating and splashing in the water, enjoying herself. Then she got out of the flotation device and began to swim by herself without the support. She was so happy—she was so happy that she finally got to float by herself and swim! As that memory came back to her, she smiled, and all of a sudden, she felt as if there was a flotation device of light around her; her arms just relaxed and rested, and all the pain completely melted away. For the next several minutes, she could do this Qigong movement with comfort and ease. Her Qi field was holding her up, and she was so grateful.

There was another woman at the retreat who was a little bit hyper. I did not like her energy, but she kept trying to talk to me. I thought, "I don't want to interact with this person. Leave me alone, I'm trying to heal." But guess what? When it came time to gather in our small discussion groups, she was in my group! And that made me smile, because I realized that was exactly perfect. I had thought, "Well, gosh, I would kind of like to go to a different group—I know I don't want to be in the same group as this person." But I just decided to go with: "Everything is perfect as it is, and there is a purpose to everything; there is a reason I am with this woman."

And the reason was that this was an opportunity for me to look at my own judgments instead of just giving in to them; I opened myself up to the possibility of learning. And 'lo and behold,' during our sharing time she talked about all of her struggles with pain and suffering and illness along with her weight issues. It broke my heart, and my heart opened to compassion.

I thought how silly my judgment was, because here is this being who is suffering, and she was just trying her best to find home—to find healing. So I really saw her in that moment as someone just like me and just like you and just like all of us. We all have similar suffering in our lives, and we deal with it in different ways. Some of us become depressed or angry; some of us become hyper and isolated. We all deal with suffering in different ways, but at the core there is still suffering. We are just being our human selves.

So I was grateful that she was in my group, because she helped open my heart to the truth of our humanity and our solidarity and allowed me to open to compassion.

Compassion and Support for the Struggling

There was so much love and compassion and support to help me get through the retreat.

One of the assistant teachers helped me get a ride to Whole Foods, so I could get some organic things to help me with my health. She even gave me her special fluffy pillow so I could sleep better at night, and she let me borrow her pad so I could lie down on the floor during some of the sessions. Sometimes during the lectures, I was so exhausted; I just wanted to lie down. When one is detoxing through Qigong, the body gets tired.

One young woman noticed that I had a cold which was from detoxing and processing things out. She asked, "Do you have a cold, sweetie? Let me get you a cup of hot tea." And so she did, and that was so sweet.

I had a one-on-one session with the Qigong master, and for half an hour he was sending me Qi energy—healing, chanting, and guiding me through meditation. A young man who brought his guitar to the retreat asked if it would be okay to sing a song for me at the beginning of my treatment. So he sang a song for me. He made up a song, a sweet song, on the guitar and sang it to me.

The Qigong master and his wife had a little two-year-old baby running around, and he was so cute; and there were other children. There were cups of tea, and there was a beautiful young man serenading me; and there were special pillows—so much support in this universe! If only we would be more open to it, we would see it. It is always there, but when we are so focused on our own problems, we do not see all of the support that is constantly there.

Smell The Flowers

There is a saying: "Stop and smell the flowers."

When we are going through disease, tragedy, suffering, or crisis in our lives, it is important not to get sucked into a black hole, as if it is the only thing that exists. Remember to smell the flowers. So yes, I am going through cancer. And I say, "So what?" It is just one of many things in this amazingly crazy, wondrous universe. So what else is there besides cancer? *Oh yes, there are flowers!*

What is Really There?

There is a Zen story of a man who is walking through the wilderness, and all of a sudden there are tigers that appear. They start to chase him, so he begins to run; he runs to a cliff and climbs down the cliff onto a branch of a tree, and he is just hanging there. The tiger is up above, and down below is a raging river. If he falls, he will fall to his death; if he goes back up, the tiger will eat him. But in front of him, as he is holding on to the branch, he sees a wild strawberry. He looks up at the tiger, and he looks down at the raging, flooding river; then he just picks the strawberry and eats it. *Yum*!

Yes, there are tigers in life. Yes there are flooding rivers in life too. But in this present moment, there is a strawberry waiting. There is a flower waiting. So do not let the regrets of the past pull you down, and do not let the worries of the future drown you. Stay in the present moment here and now and realize the gift that is right here, right before you and within you and all around.

A Meditation on Life, Death & Resurrection-Part Two
April 20, 2014-Dallas, Texas

Easter Is

On Easter, Christians celebrate the death and resurrection of Jesus, but I view it in another broader way. Jesus is a great Bodhisattva of Love, and the point of Jesus' story is in the way He lived His life as a Bodhisattva of Love.

But unfortunately over the centuries, religious dogmatic fundamentalists have truncated the point of his message. The meaning they have assigned to Jesus is only that He was born on Christmas with all these angels and shepherds doing stuff and that He died and rose again at the end. They rarely talk about everything in between, which is actually the whole point of why He came. He did not feel any shame being with the "riffraff," and He just loved partying with the common people, and not just the elite. He treated women as equals; He treated children with sacred love and respect. He healed people with His love, encouraging them that it is their faith that makes them whole.

The Great Example Rather Than The Great Exception

Jesus reminds us that we have power within us already and that we do not have to beg some external divine power for our healing. It is our faith that makes us whole. He said that we too can do all of the great and wonderful things that He had done, even greater than He, if we just have enough faith: "All these wonderful things you see me do, you can do also; even greater than what I've done." But the religious dogmatic fundamentalists over the centuries have put him on this high, high pedestal, where basically He is not even the same species as us. I believe He is the great exception rather than the great example, but not because He had some miraculous virgin birth, died and miraculously rose from the dead physically; that is not the point. The point is everything in between. I believe He is the great exception rather than the great example because His message was in his example, in the way He lived and spoke, in the way He touched people and interacted with them.

Power of Light

Jesus lived His life, radiated love, and healed others by having faith in people's faith. And so, I celebrate Easter not because He died for my sins, but that in every situation, even at the end, nothing could overcome His light—no amount of suffering, no amount of ignorance, no amount of opposition, no amount of crucifixion could snuff out His light. So the point of Easter is not about the suffering; we all have suffering. The point is that you can overcome anything and everything because you have the light in you, and no amount of complication or suffering or tribulation or trial or crisis can ever, ever put out your light.

We are the light of the world, and Jesus is not the only one who demonstrated that; Buddha did too, as have many, many people in history. You are demonstrating it in your life as well. Look at all the suffering you have gone through in this life, and you are still here—you are still growing; you are still evolving; and you are still shining your light. It is amazing how much you have gone through; and yet, you are still here shining your light. You are each a testimony to Buddha's nature, to Christ's nature, to God's nature, to Spirit's nature. All of us are beautiful testimonies of the light: "We are the resurrection and the life." That is the meaning of the Jesus story.

The Second Coming

When I think about what the second coming of Christ means, I don't imagine some physical Jesus coming out of the sky in a spaceship. That is not the real meaning of the second coming. The second coming is a spiritual event—the spiritualization of human consciousness on the earth. It is an understanding of the real meaning of the first coming of Christ when more and more people will start realizing that it is not about worshiping a man named Jesus, but about following what He was all about and getting in touch with the same divine consciousness. If we can get in touch with that same divine consciousness, we can start allowing that light to shine the way Jesus let his light shine, the way Buddha and others let their lights shine. That will be the second coming of Christ on a global scale.

When people start waking up and becoming enlightened, they will begin to transform the world. They will start to realize that it is not about putting some other person on a pedestal or an altar, but it is about how we can let that light shine collectively and globally. That is the second coming of Christ, and it is already starting to happen. It has been happening for centuries and is starting to intensify, and now it is exponential.

I believe that the years from 2020 to 2060 are going to be explosive years of spiritual evolution, and I don't think that when we get to 2060 we are going to even recognize our planet. It is going to be so amazing. Does that mean it is going to be all flowers and gardens? No, not necessarily. I think there will be a lot of crazy changes on earth with political and economic crises, etc.—all kinds of crazy stuff will happen. But in the midst of that, our light, our inner light, will continue to shine and grow. More and more people are going to realize the real meaning of Christ, the real meaning of Buddha, and the real meaning of spirituality.

For more insight and information, I highly recommend a book by Richard Hooper titled *Jesus, Buddha, Krishna, and Lao-Tzu: The Parallel Sayings*. He takes the different teachings of each of these four great masters and shows how their messages are very similar.

Another book I recommend is by one of my favorite spiritual teachers Adyashanti, *Resurrecting Jesus: Embodying the Spirit of a Revolutionary Mystic*. Adyashanti is a Zen Buddhist spiritual teacher, but he takes his Zen spiritual understanding and looks at the life of Jesus, seeing it through a Zen lens. It is a spiritual, interfaith alliance. I especially love the first chapters where he tells a personal story about his own spiritual journey in Buddhist meditation, as well as appreciating and having his heart break open by the Christ consciousness.

And although we all read books, we have to remember to stop reading and start practicing. At some point we have to stop reading about meditating and actually meditate.

Amen.

Universe in Harmonious Meditation   Sakshi Agarwal

Mindfulness, Buddha, Love, And Emotions

November 10, 2013-St. Paul, Minnesota; Clouds in Water Zen Center

Recently I discovered a book by a Japanese Tendai priest that recounts her near-death experience. She used to live in California and now lives in Japan.

> Brother ChiSing SIDE BAR:
>
> In the Tendai tradition of Buddhism, there is a focus on the Lotus Sutra, but there are many practices that are cultivated and that are possible. Many famous Buddhist teachers used to be Tendai priests. The Pure Land teacher, the Nichiren teacher, and also Dogen, a Zen teacher, came from the Tendai tradition.

In her near death experience, she started seeing herself in this beautiful place by a river, and there were two boats. Many people were getting into one boat, and in the other boat, there were Buddhas and bodhisattvas. One of the Buddhas waved to her to come into their boat, and she felt so happy to be able to be in the company of such beautiful beings. They asked her to sit on a beautiful lotus seat in the boat, but as she got on the boat, she realized that her work was not quite finished on Earth. There were still many people that needed help from her, including her family. So she bowed to the Buddhas and humbly declined saying, "Please come back for me later after I have done my work." Then she found herself once again in the hospital, in a state of awakened consciousness.

I like sharing her story because it serves as a reminder to all of us that not only Christians or certain others can have near-death experiences; everyone can—including Buddhists. There was a Christian minister, a hospital chaplain named John W. Price who had visited with people on their deathbed and listened to their stories. Many of those who had come back from death recounted to him what they had seen and experienced. He wrote hundreds of cases in his book titled *Revealing Heaven: The Christian Case for Near-Death Experiences*.

After hearing hundreds of stories, he was shocked to learn that not only were Christians seeing heavenly visions but non-Christians, too. God forbid! And a few of them were even gay or lesbian. They saw a life review of all the skillful and unskillful things that had been in their actions, and being gay or lesbian was not an issue at all. It was more about: "How much did you love?" "How much did you learn to receive love?"

But what shocked him the most was the story of two very conservative ministers who had died, had come back, and were themselves in shock by what they had seen. All of their lives, they had preached on hell fire, brimstone, damnation, and the wrath of God; but when they came back, they realized that none of that existed in the heavenly realm, none of this judgment, only love. They realized that only love is at the core of our existence. When they realized how wrong they had been in the way that they had approached religion, they tried to change their message, but after a few months they were fired from their church. The people just could not stand hearing about love, light, acceptance and tolerance.

We Come From Wisdom And Compassion

You know, it is because of our existence in the reality of love that we can focus on this present moment. We do not have to worry about our origins. Our origins are wisdom and compassion—that is where we come from. We do not have to worry about where we are going either; there is love and light always embracing us. So if we do not need to worry about our past, and we do not need to worry about our future, then we can now focus on what we are here for, just in this present moment.

As we practice mindfulness and awareness, being present here and now, we can begin having mindfulness with our body. Mindfulness of our breath really is a wonderful way of being present with our body. But we can also be mindful of our feelings. Our feelings have two aspects: they can be either physical or emotional. The more physical feelings would be sensations, for example, like a little bit of itchy feeling or soreness. I do not have to call it an 'evil' itch or 'evil' backache or 'evil' foot falling asleep, because no, it is not that. Instead of instantly labeling everything with judgment, just be with the sensation as it is without labeling it as these very controversial kinds of judgments.

We can also be mindful of the other aspect of feelings, which is more on the side of our mind, more about our emotions. Eventually we can be mindful of our mind, be more mindful about how our mind works, and try to see through our mind. We can have mindfulness of all of the reality and truth of how things truly operate in the universe.

Love, Peace, Joy Vs. Anger, Fear, Sadness

In the last few weeks I have been meditating on the energy centers in the lower abdomen, the heart area, and in the head. Traditionally, in Chinese philosophy we believe that the energy center in the abdomen corresponds to our connection with the earth energy—harmony with the earth and the physical body. The heart is our connection to our emotions and our humanity. The head energy center connects us to the heaven energy and spirit energy, as well as cosmic energy. When we are balanced in these energies, in harmony with heaven and earth and humanity, then we are being mindful.

As I was being mindful of these energy centers, I was thinking about our emotions, and I thought of the three primary positive emotions. In the heart is *love* which, of course, makes sense to me. In the lower abdomen, well, that is the center of vitality, and so I thought *joy*. And in the head, when my mind is calm, I have *peace*.

But as I continued to contemplate these positive emotions, I realized that is not all that exists in the human condition. We also have what we might consider negative emotions which correspond to these energy centers of positive emotions. Anger corresponds with love; sadness corresponds with joy; and fear corresponds with peace. There are the bad emotions on one side, and there are the good emotions on the other side. Right?

We have love, peace, and joy, and we also have anger, fear, and sadness. At first I thought, okay, these are the good emotions, the others are the bad emotions; but they are actually all valid. They are all part of the human condition, and they all have healthy places in our lives.

Sometimes we have fear, especially if a lion is chasing us, but I do not know how often that happens to us. Sometimes we can feel anger, perhaps at injustice, and sadness is very normal, especially when we are grieving. So these are all healthy emotions. Suppressing what we think of as negative emotions can actually cause unhealthy forms of these emotions to manifest.

For instance, if we are not mindful enough, fear can lead to extremes of anxiety and paranoia. Anger can lead toward unhealthy extremes of hatred, rage, and revenge. And sadness can lead to debilitating depression, etc. So we need to be mindful of our emotions, to express them in healthy ways and bring them back to health when they become unhealthy.

The Other Side of Peace, Love And Joy

So-called negative emotions can be expressed in extreme and unhealthy ways, but so can the so-called positive emotions. If we do not know how to cultivate and nourish the positive side of these emotions, there can be unhealthy expressions as well.

Being at peace in an unhealthy expression might manifest into uncaring apathy, indifference, and laziness. And love, oh my goodness, who thought love could have an unhealthy side? But it really can. Love can manifest into obsessive-compulsive possessiveness and into lusting, craving, and clinging. Joy can become manic or frenzied or irresponsible fun, fun gone wild that is out of control. And that may be very harmful to people.

Mindfulness extends into many different areas, and as we practice mindfulness, it allows us to have insight and wisdom as to what is skillfully working for us and what is not.

Thank you so much for your practice.

The Wandering Mind

October 6, 2009-Letter To The Sangha

Editor's Note: This was not a formal talk but a written letter.

It might sometimes be difficult to meditate because your mind wanders so much. Your thoughts begin to race in all directions; concentration and focus are hard. Yet, is it not true that your mind is usually in this state? But when you sit down on your meditation seat, you have the opportunity to see what is really going on.

Meditation is not the cause of your wandering mind; meditation simply allows you to see what is already there. Meditation is a way of stopping and observing. And what you most often see at first may not be pleasant, but if you do not face the reality of what has been going on for so long—namely, a mind that is out of control—you will not be able to transform yourself and awaken to your True Nature.

Sit With What Is

What is needed is courage of the heart to face the current situation of the untransformed mind and to sit with it as it is, as well as faith to trust that awareness itself is already transformative. Instead of resisting and resenting the wandering mind during meditation, simply watch without judgment the tangled workings of the mind. Your anchor is mindfulness of the present moment and perhaps of the body sitting here and now, breathing in and breathing out.

During your meditation practice:

- Be aware of a thought, noting the kind of thought it is, and then come back to the breath in the body, to this present moment.

- Be aware of a sound, noting the tonal quality of the sound, and then come back to the breath in the body, to this present moment.

- Be aware of a sensation on the skin or in the body, noting the details of the sensation without adding thoughts and interpretive judgments onto it, and then come back to the breath in the body, to this present moment.

- Be aware of a feeling or emotion, noting whether it is pleasant, unpleasant or neutral, perhaps labeling the feeling without getting pulled into the mental and emotional drama of it, and then come back to the breath in the body, to this present moment.

- Be aware of planning mind, aware of memory mind, aware of worry mind; be aware of judging mind, drowsy mind, hyperactive mind, day dreaming mind, and then, each time, come back to this present moment, to the breath in the here and now, again and again.

Eventually, you will notice certain patterns, mind-habits, and connections between thoughts and feelings. You will begin to realize how impermanent and insubstantial your thoughts are, how your feelings are multi-layered and malleable, and how you constantly identify who you are with your ever-shifting mind states and life dramas, when in fact—"You are not your mind!"

And furthermore, you are not your addictions. You are not your accomplishments. You are not your self-esteem (high or low). You are not your I.Q.

Much suffering stems from the false identification of thoughts and feelings (the human story) with our True Nature. The body and mind are impermanent; they are not who you ultimately are, and to believe and act otherwise leads to suffering. *Who then are you?*

You Are A Buddha

Who then are you? The answer is that you are a Buddha. To know this and to live in this realization is Nirvana. As you awaken to the Truth of who you are, the mind is no longer simply the mind but is the 'mind of the Buddha' (bodhicitta), and the body is no longer simply the body but is the 'body of the Buddha' (buddhakaya). Both body and mind, then, are understood in their true light as tools of exploration, vehicles of expression—skillful means (upaya) and not ends in and of themselves.

The Zen Of Messy Enlightenment-Part One

March 3, 2015-Houston, Texas, Unity of Houston

The Zen of messy enlightenment is the only kind I know as I have been on an amazing but crazy wonderful journey this past year. About a year ago, I found out that I have a rare form of nasal cancer—or had; that is how I like to think of it. And I chose to keep practicing everything I had already been practicing throughout it all. Amazingly, within a very short time, I found myself in a state of consciousness where I was able to touch very deeply a place of peace and non-fear. And I believe it is because of all of my years of spiritual practice.

If you wait until you have a crisis to perform spiritual practices, then it is a little too late, and not because it is actually too late; it is never really too late. But when you are in a crisis, spiritual practice is sometimes the last thing you think about or have the energy to do. So I recommend that you start deepening all of your spiritual practices now, including meditation, so that you are more prepared for whatever is to come. Because of my spiritual practice, I was able to really go through this process with much more of a sense of peace and non-fear.

Feel The Fear—Do It Anyway

Non-fear does not mean that you do not have days of fear; it means that you do not allow the fear to dominate and overwhelm you. You know, it is like that saying, "Feel the fear and do it anyway." So it is not that I do not have fear sometimes, but that underlying courage, confidence, hope, and peace is always there throughout the ups and downs of normal human emotion.

This past year, I decided to treat my body, mind, heart, and spirit to fullness of health and not worry so much about this so-called disease. I did not want to keep thinking about it all the time. Instead, I thought about all kinds of other wonderful things in life. In fact, there have been some days when I did not even remember I had cancer. And I think that is a good way to practice, because otherwise you are focusing too much on the so-called problem.

The way I was guided to treat myself to health was through a very integrative holistic approach where I combined every possible, conceivable modality that you can think of: prayer, meditation, spiritual healing and spiritual mind treatment, a little bit of conventional therapy, alternative therapies, homeopathy, and Chinese medicine. You name it; I have done it. And it paid off because my first original tumor is gone. I just have this smaller secondary tumor behind my right eye that is still there, but I know it is shrinking, and I am really grateful. By the time the summer comes, I am very hopeful that it will be all gone.

In the past year of practicing spiritual audacity, I have become aware of a lot of deep insights. One of the interesting things, as we have all heard, is that when we go through some sort of crisis, there are many deep spiritual gifts that may occur. I had always heard that, but now I know it is true.

Health Opportunity

In fact, a few years ago, I wondered what my midlife crisis would be like in my forties. Well here it is. And instead of being a problem, it is a wonderful opportunity. Instead of calling my—this disease of cancer as mine, I am naming it a health opportunity.

That is something that I learned when I went into retreat this past year, where they specialize on how to support your own healing process. Going to healing retreats, like the Optimum Health Institute in Austin, reminded me that I am not alone, and instead of seeing this as a problem, it was a health opportunity.

I have grown so much in the past year—so exponentially—that looking back I believe that my soul chose to allow myself to go through this as a way for me to grow. Now that does not mean that everything is necessarily for that purpose. You know, I am not going to say, "Oh, that person is going through this because of such and such." I do not have any right to say anything about another person's life. But for me, as I have meditated and reflected, I know that this was definitely part of my soul process. And so I look forward to the second half of my life now, alive and well, and to becoming a better spiritual teacher and sharing the light with many more people.

I went to a clinic in Arizona where they specialize in alternative, integrative medical therapies. I was there for 40 days and 40 nights. I decided I was going 40 days and 40 nights, because if it was good enough for Jesus, then it was good enough for me.

Mindfulness For Me Too

After a few weeks of driving to the clinic every day, I was thinking to myself about how I am always telling people about mindfulness and how we should be mindful throughout the day, not just when we are meditating. And then I thought to myself, "Oh, maybe I should practice that, too!" So, I decided I would be very mindful as I drove to the clinic that day, and as I did, I noticed for the first time the three main roads that I had been taking the whole time. I had never really noticed or paid attention to them. But when I thought about it, I realized the names of the roads were: Alma School Road, University Avenue, and Center Street.

And in that moment, a spark of joy lit up my heart as I realized that the divine universe was sending a message to me and was waiting for me to be mindful enough to pay attention. There is a lesson here, a lesson of encouragement and affirmation. Alma in Spanish means soul, so Alma School means soul school. I realized that this healing journey that I am on right now is a part of my soul school experience. It is not an accident; it is not some tragedy where I am a victim. No, it is part of my soul school training. And University Avenue—well, I was at a higher level than usual. I was definitely going through a disease or crisis, and it was not a kindergarten experience—let me tell you. But this was a challenge that I was definitely ready for at the university level of spirit.

And Center Street—I realized that the main theme of this whole lesson is for me to grow and to learn how to stay centered in the truth of who I really am in the midst of circumstances saying otherwise: the truth that 'I am always loved, I am always safe, and I am always free, no matter what.'

So having been to all of the hospitals and the clinics and the retreats, I have started to realize that I am not alone. The divine is always with me, in me, as me; and not only the divine as ultimate spirit, but also the divine in you, in me, in everyone around me is on this journey with me.

We are all on this journey together. Are we not all on a healing journey, in body, in mind, and in spirit?

The Zen Of Messy Enlightenment-Part Two

March 3, 2015-Houston, Texas, Unity of Houston

We really have only three missions in this lifetime; it simply boils down to just that. So when someone asks, "What is my mission in life?" Here is the answer:

First, we are meant to find our spiritual elders and learn from them, receive from them, honor them, respect them, and be grateful for them. We have so many enlightened teachers on the planet today, more now than ever before. It would be so sad if we did not take advantage and receive from them. So please find them; find who they are. For me, one of them is Thich Nhat Hanh, and I am so grateful that I was able to receive from him. If I had not, then I would not be sitting here before you today. So find your spiritual elders and support them and listen to them.

The second mission in life is to find your younger spiritual brothers and sisters and be of service to them, because people who are young souls suffer a lot. They make a lot of choices that are not always helpful, so they need older brothers and sisters like us to be of service to them. And that does not mean to control or fix them; it just means to be present for them.

And then the third mission in life is to find your spiritual peers, people who are basically more or less your equals in soul growth, and create wonderful things in life with them—relationships, friendships, churches, communities, projects. Create wonderful, wonderful things in life with your fellow brothers and sisters.

There Is A Fourth Mission

As I reflected on these insights that had come to me this past year, a fourth mission came to me last month. The fourth mission is to let go of those who are not meant to be in your life right now. You have your spiritual elders, your spiritual younger brothers and sisters, and your spiritual peers, but there are also people who are just not meant to be in your sphere of influence at this time, in this lifetime.

So just bless them, and let them go. You do not need to make yourself suffer over and over and over again by wishing them to be in your life when they really are not. They used to be in your life, but they no longer want to be there. *So why are you doing that to yourself?* Human life is so short, and there are so many other things to do with the other three missions. Do not make the mistake of being attached to people who are not meant to really stay in your life. Just let them go and bless them.

There are seven billion other people on the planet that would love to spend time with you. Maybe you have something wonderful to share with someone, but you are unable to share it with them because you are so stuck on a few people who are not really meant to be in your life. So just let them go.

I invite you to check out these wonderful books:

Dying to Be Me: My Journey from Cancer to Near Death to True Healing by Anita Moorjani is a wonderful and encouraging book. A brief synopsis is that basically after she died from all these cancerous tumors, she saw heaven and angelic guides and was given the choice to go back or stay. She did not want to go back, and I am not surprised, because it is so great there in heaven. But the angelic guides persuaded her by saying, "You have a mission to complete, and if you go back, you can complete that mission and help many, many souls. When you go back, all of your cancer tumors will completely melt away in one week." And that is exactly what happened as verified by the doctors. So now she is fulfilling her mission. She is telling her story and sharing workshops on the power and truth that death is not real.

Another book by Thich Nhat Hanh, my teacher, is *No Death, No Fear*. What a wonderful blessing that book has been for me this last year! Also, Derek Rydall's new book *Emergence: Seven Steps for Radical Life Change* is going to be a bestseller in all the New Thought communities. Basically, the premise of this book is that instead of practicing what is usually called self-help, as if you are just this awful thing and you need to be improved, think of it more as that there is already perfection within you wanting to emerge and unfold. It is a very different way of looking at change—radical change.

Be Still And Know

August 19, 2007-Dallas, Texas

Editor's Note: This is the first recorded dharma talk given by Brother ChiSing at the Awakening Heart Sunday meditation group in Dallas.

I just came back from a retreat that was themed mindfulness, fearlessness, and togetherness. And on the altar, written in calligraphy with large letters was: "Be still and know." Those of us with knowledge of the Western spiritual traditions know that these words come from the book of Psalms in the Bible: "Be still and know."

This simple verse actually outlines the whole of Buddhist meditation practice. The *still* is an aspect of meditation called Samatha, which is stopping, calming, and concentrating. The Samatha breathing method of counting the breath helps beginners to concentrate and focus: "Breathing in, one, breathing out, one; breathing in, two, breathing out, two; breathing in, three, breathing out, three; and so forth, until 10, and then start again at one, one, two, two, etc."

Lost Count?

But if you find yourself at 11 and 12, you know that you are getting lost because the counting is just automatic rather than completely conscious; and if you notice that, just start again at one. And if you are at five and start thinking about the recipe for tomorrow's lunch and you realize, "Oh, I don't know what breath I am on," then just come back to one again. There is no judgment; just come back to one. This is called Samatha.

And another aspect of meditation is called Vipassana, which means to look deeply, to concentrate and look deeply into the nature of reality and *know*. We start by focusing on things that are easy, such as looking deeply into the nature of the body and its form and looking deeply into our organs and all the different parts that make up our body. Then move to sensations on our skin, our feelings from emotions, and then move onto our mental states and thoughts and the way our mind works. Then, from there we begin to know the reality of the whole universe and the spiritual teachings and how they relate to the truth of reality as it is.

So 'be still and know.' Be *still* and *know*—both help us to let go of all that obstructs us from just being naturally and radiantly who we already are which is wisdom, insight, understanding and truth. Of course that is just one angle of the Buddhist meditation practice; another one is that we are also love, compassion, joy, and forgiveness. In fact, in Buddhism, these two aspects of our awakened nature are expressed as such: wisdom and compassion; they are never separate. There is no true wisdom without compassion and love, and there is no true love and compassion without understanding and wisdom. So 'be still and know'—be still, be calm, concentrate and focus. Be present here and now in meditation through the breath, through visualization, or through whatever works for you; it really does not matter. The point is to be really here and now in this moment so that the light we bring is not diffused like a weak light bulb, but concentrated like a laser where all the light beams are going in the same direction. And because of that concentration, that Samatha, we can look deeply and truly allow insight to awaken naturally—insight into the nature of the universe, into the nature of our suffering, into the nature of our true happiness.

Distracting Thich Nhat Hanh

During the second day of the retreat, Thich Nhat Hanh shared a story about his time in Korea where thousands and thousands of people were trying to touch him and take pictures of him while he was trying to lead a walking meditation outside in public. As soon as he started to walk, crowds of people just started to come in, and reporters were flashing their cameras; and it was not a very mindful atmosphere. It must have been very distracting, probably very much like hearing the ticking of a clock, only multiplied 100 times along with the flashing cameras. So you can imagine that it might drive someone a little bit crazy. He was feeling frustrated and exasperated and thought this is just impossible.

And he just closed his eyes, took a deep breath and said, "Okay. Buddha, you have to walk for me." And in a few seconds, he felt the energy of the universe, of his true nature, just expressing through his body and mind. And he took the first step, and the crowds just naturally and effortlessly parted—kind of like Moses and the Red Sea. And he just walked; and it was a wonderful walk, very peaceful, very solid, very joyful, and very mindful.

And so he wrote this gatha or poem called "Breathing and Walking." And when I heard it from his mouth, it touched my heart, and I just felt this wonderful feeling of truth. Because he was distracted, he let the Buddha breathe and walk. The poem relates the realization that he himself did not need to do that; the Buddha could do the breathing and walking. There is no breather. There is no walker. There is just breathing and walking.

And he could enjoy the walking meditation in peace and joy.

So there is no breather, just breathing—no walker, just walking. And so there is just singing; there is no singer, just singing. There is no thinker, just thinking. There is no feeler, just feeling. There is no sufferer, just suffering. There is no awakener, just awakening, just everything flowing, being, dancing—just like a candle, everything extinguishing moment to moment, letting go moment to moment, to manifest moment to moment just this breathing, just this walking, just this singing, just this thinking and feeling and moving and smiling and being.

Willingness, Willfulness (Dharma Potpourri)

August 31, 2008-Dallas, Texas

I was not really sure what I wanted to talk about tonight; I was thinking of maybe just making kind of a dharma potpourri. Sometimes I call it a dharma collage, and when I am really not thinking of any particular themes, the dharma potpourri.

So, as I was sitting in the chapel, meditating a little bit before we started tonight, I was thinking about some of the things that I had learned at the retreat that I had just been to in California. One thing that I had learned was not to look for the truth in the future or somewhere other than right here and right now. So, sitting in the chapel tonight, I asked myself, "Okay, well, so what's the truth, right here and right now?

And when I opened my eyes I noticed two words on a stained glass window in the chapel: *will* and *understanding*—just those two words. To come to a place of deep wisdom and understanding, I needed to look at this thing called 'the will,' because control issues are a pretty major thing in my life, and it may be for some of you too. For me, when I feel that energy of control in my body, it feels as if it is right in my stomach area and has a kind of jaggedness to it, an intention. I know it is always there, and I know it is a major issue for me. It was one of the issues that was addressed at the retreat.

While each of us have our own different issues that we are dealing with, mine was starkly evident to me towards the end of the retreat when I had noticed that I no longer felt the jaggedness; there was just a smoothness. There was no longer a need for me to control anything, but to just be with everything just as it is. No longer was I complaining about the heat or bothered by my position on the cushion or by the fly tickling me. In that place of surrender, I thought to myself, "Oh wow!" I suddenly realized how much time I had spent not allowing myself to surrender fully because I had been so used to that jaggedness and had not been sure the smoothness was there.

Resistance Is Futile...

Willingness is our practice. And when we observe that we are not willing—meaning not allowing or not being—then we may observe that we are being willful or resisting. At the entrance to the retreat, there was a big sign that read, "Resistance is Futile," and it became our mantra for the week. There is a major difference between feelings of willingness and feelings of willfulness. So when we observe that there is willfulness, we do not need to resist that because it just feeds it.

For example, if you find yourself saying, "Oh I'm feeling irritated," or "I'm feeling upset," and you get upset or irritated at the upsetness and irritation, then you are feeding it, and that is not helpful. Just say to yourself, "There is some willfulness here," and then be willing to be with that willfulness, so that the willfulness will just naturally show you what it needs to show you and then dissipate.

Willingness Practice Presents Itself

I had an opportunity right after the retreat to practice this as I was still in a very smooth, peaceful, equanimous state of consciousness and just kind of being with things as they are. I drove to Oakland to check out the place where I used to live because I had left several hundred books with some of my previous roommates and friends to care for them because they loved my books and wanted them around. Over the last three years, roommates had come and gone, but it had been okay because last year their friends had been living there and were totally loving the books too. But when I arrived, the people that were living there now unkindly remarked, "So you're the one with all the books! We haven't known what to do with these books for all these months and finally you show up!" They told me that because I had left the books they now belonged to them, and I did not have any right to take them back—these are hundreds of dollars, maybe thousands of dollars worth of books.

I was kind of shocked by the hostility, and so in that moment I remembered I could choose to be either willing or willful and let that teach me what it needed to teach me and then dissipate. I could choose to say or do something in reaction; then I would have to deal with that emotion for many minutes or hours later, maybe even longer. Up to that point, I had been saying to myself, "Okay, willing,

willing, willing," but I was so startled by the hostility that I just reacted: "Well, those are my books, and they're worth a lot of money and how dare you!"

And because I chose to go with that, I felt all of this stuff inside, and it took me a while to work through that. So I went to a park in San Francisco and did some walking meditation. At a little Catholic convent there, I went inside the chapel, sat for a few minutes while thinking about the experience and remembered what I had learned at the retreat. Instead of adding to the problem by being willful with the willfulness, I decided to just willingly say to myself, "Okay, I was a little willful." So what is the lesson here? The lesson is that I can learn from the willingness, because within minutes, instead of hours or days, it just dissipated. Willingness taught me what it needed to teach me, that I needed to be willing to be with my willfulness; and I was able to just let it go and go forward from there.

Intention And Manifesting

Now those of you who are into New Thought, like Unity teachings or Science of Mind teachings, might be asking yourselves, "Well, where does intention and manifesting come into play? Where does that fit into willingness and into letting things be as they are?" Well, as I was meditating during the retreat, I had an insight, and this insight that had come to me may not necessarily be the absolute truth. But what came to me is that both are valid truths; they are both valid in a certain way together.

Obviously, if you go the extreme of letting things be just as they are or just being with things as they are, and if you are doing it from the kind of angle that it is an excuse to be lazy or an excuse to not care about what happens in the world, then you may want to look at that again and see if it is really the truth. Yet, at the other extreme are people who are into manifestations and who are scared and think that something bad is going to happen if they are not thinking every single thought positively or if they do not make the will and effort and intention. They experience a lot of struggling and striving in their lives and have a lot of anxiety.

Perhaps we lightly hold a positive intention. Maybe that positive intention is about healing the past and finding peace in the present, or maybe it is about seeking harmony with others in the future or with our planet for the future. Whatever that positive intention is, lightly hold it in the spacious center of a sense of allowing, a sense of innocent wonder, a sense of life simply unfolding moment by moment or moment to moment, perfect just as it is, no need to control—breathing in, breathing out, *ahhh*. So yes, have your positive intention of what you want to manifest in your life, but hold it lightly in a spacious center aware of allowing and of wonder so you can ask yourself, "Okay now what's going to happen?" *You see?* It's like that! Oh, what an interesting experiment life is, what an interesting adventure life is!

Thy Will Be Done

There is a very famous phrase from Christ's prayer that reads, "Thy will be done on Earth as it is in Heaven." And I saw insight into the entire Lord's Prayer of how each phrase is going back and forth between being-ness and the expression of being-ness. "Thy will be done"—that phrase was so powerful for me. *Thy will...*; the truth will be expressed—being doing, being feeling, being thinking, being expressed. So, when I used to hear the words, "Thy will be done," I would have a sort of cringing feeling—*Oh my God! Okay! Thy will be done!*

But the insight that arose in me was: Thy 'will' expressed as *love, peace, joy*, and 'be done' expressed as *in and through me and all beings*. So there is a sense of love and joy and peace when we say it as expressed in that way—'Thy will be done' *in me, through me, as me*. And that is willingness, willing to be willing, to allow the will of the divine of our true nature, our Buddha-nature, to be expressed in us, through us, and as us, rather than willfulness which has a sense of contraction and fear, tightness and jagged edges, and a lot of the energy of ego. But even if that is there, we can hold that with a sense of willingness.

Willing To Let The Cake Bake

At the retreat, there was a wonderful picture of a beautiful Buddha sitting in front of a body of water, and in the reflection was the Buddha's refection, but in the reflection was a clown. And so, our true nature holds and embraces everything, including the foolish aspects of ourselves. And the clown, however you might want to interpret that clown, holds everything—our humanness, our ego. Everything is held; it is included.

When we come from a place of ego, it is exclusive; it is me vs. them—it is a separation, a division. But when we are in a space of willingness and allowing of being, it has that quality of peace and love and joy. But willingness can also hold the emotions of anger, irritation and frustration; it is inclusive, rather than exclusive. And that is what I learned at the retreat, that in every moment, if I choose instantly to be willing when confronted with something, then it would just teach me what it needed to teach me and then dissipate and melt naturally. Whereas, if I did or said something in a reactive mode, it was my choice in that moment to deal with that emotion for minutes, hours, and even longer. And it is not as if I did not know that intellectually, but that is what is what a retreat is for. It is not about necessarily getting more ingredients, it is knowing that I already had them. I think most of us already have enough ingredients; we just need to let the cake bake.

The universe has already given you everything you need for peace, wisdom, love, joy; you just need to take the ingredients and let the cake bake in the oven of life. It is not always easy. But if we are willing, all those ingredients can bake into a beautiful cake We know this already in our hearts. We already have the ingredients; we just need to let our cake bake to let that manifest more full and unfold. It is just a matter of practicing every moment. We are not trying to get anywhere, because it is all here, right now.

It is funny because it is said that when you become enlightened, you realize that it has been here the whole time. It is not like you are trying to reach Nirvana. Nirvana has been living itself out in every moment—in the grass, in the little bees flying around, even in the stubbing of your toe against the table. Everything has just simply been Nirvana expressing itself, enlightenment expressing itself, Buddha expressing itself, the divine expressing itself. This is the Kingdom of Heaven; this is the Pure Land of the Buddha.

When we are in the dream world of the ego, we interpret this reality in other, different ways. We divide it into good and bad, pleasant and unpleasant, and what we want and what we don't want. But in actuality, those divisions only occur when we believe in the dream world of the ego, for when we awaken from that dream, everything is as it is, perfection itself, even what is considered imperfect. So, as each opportunity comes for us to choose, to see from the place of ego or to see from the place of the inclusive truth, in that moment we have the opportunity to make a choice. If we choose from the place of ego, then there is a problem. We think it is a problem, we feel it is a problem, and we struggle with using what was the problem to try to solve the problem. But when we choose to encounter that moment from the place of the inclusive truth, then even what might be unpleasant or difficult becomes a messenger, becomes something that will help us grow and see more deeply, and help us to bake the cake more thoroughly.

Ganesh　　　　　　　Sakshi Agarawal

Reservoirs Of Positive Energy

January 25, 2009-Dallas, Texas

During the winter break I had spent a few weeks at a couple of retreats, and they were personally symbolic for me at this time in my life. I had been feeling that I was close to a midpoint in my life, and going to a one week retreat at the Zen Center in Houston was a way for me to clear away any negative karma from the past. And I went into the monastery and was ordained temporarily as a novice monk at the Thai Buddhist Center in Arlington with the purpose of setting a good solid foundation for myself now and into the future, especially for the next four years of this wonderful new presidency until 2012. "Breathing in, yes, breathing out, we can." *Yes, we can!*

I encourage all of you to find a way to go on a retreat or create a retreat at home—to really purify, cleanse and detox from the past and to lay a strong solid spiritual foundation for now and into the future. The world is in the midst of great change, and it is only going to get more intense. And so the world needs you and me to be mindful, to be open-minded, and to be able to release past attachments.

I shared with some people in my life that I have been feeling more and more drained for the last several months. When I first started practicing it was as if I must have been practicing in past lives because there was just so much energy, as if there was a big reservoir of energy to support me. And then over the years and especially in the last months I have felt like, perhaps, I have been running out of reserves.

Filling The Reservoirs

But after these past few weeks of practice, I am amazed that I am feeling all of this energy—this large reserve, a reservoir of positive energy once again. And when I had to speak this morning it was like it was just all there—it was effortless. It was as if I could let the Buddha breathe; I could let the Buddha talk. And even now, not so much effort is needed. I think that what I have learned during this time is the importance of creating that reservoir of positive energy. If we do not have a large reservoir of that positive energy it will be very difficult to practice meditation, to share spirituality with our loved ones and friends, and to engage in our daily lives in a mindful way. It will be very difficult and a struggle; it is a lot of energy. But when we have that reservoir of positive energy backing us up it is so much easier, and there is more gracefulness to it.

Now, how do you create that reservoir of positive energy? Well, traditionally in the Buddhist tradition, and of course in others as well, the practice of generosity and giving to those who are spiritual givers is one major way. In Buddhism we call it creating 'merit,' but I do not necessarily think that word means much to us, so that is why I am using the phrase "reservoir of positive energy." When people give food to the monks and nuns and give to the spiritual temple to support their spiritual activities, it creates great 'merit,' a great reservoir of positive energy. Even a bow to someone who is a spiritual person in service to other beings creates wonderful positive energy—even just one bow.

Fill It By Giving It

In some ways it is better to support and give to someone such as a monk, a nun or a spiritual giver, someone who gives to the world. It is almost better to do that than to give to someone who is not giving at all to the world. Now I am not saying you should choose between the two; of course we should help those who are in need. But why would I say that helping someone who is a giver will create more positive energy? Well, because when you give to someone who needs your help but whose lifestyle is not very conducive to creating much of a positive effect in the world at this time, then many times it only helps them and does not go any further than that.

But if you help someone who supports, empowers, and gives to others, then you are also giving to all the others that this person is supporting, and that is why I say that. Now do not take my words the wrong way. I still believe we have to help all those who are in need of our help. This is what the Buddha said to his students: "Please don't be jealous that I am giving more attention and time and effort and teaching to those who are on the bodhisattva path than to those who are on the non-bodhisattva path." What he meant was those students on the bodhisattva path did not seek enlightenment just for themselves, but so that they could build spiritual skills that would enable them to help many others become enlightened as well. And then those students on the non-bodhisattva path were basically doing pretty good just to try and become enlightened for themselves with not much thought given to helping other beings.

Please support those who are doing spiritual work that is beneficial to the world. Support monks and nuns, support sanghas, and support organizations that do a lot of good work in the world. And of course, support, one on one, those you meet along the way who just need a helping hand, because you never know if they might actually be a bodhisattva or an angel in disguise.

Importance Of Meditation

Another way, traditionally, that we create 'merit' or this reservoir of positive energy is through the practice of the mindfulness trainings. We do this by intentionally making vows of practicing the mindfulness training of non-violence, non-stealing, sexual responsibility, mindful speech, mindful consumption and of living by them. And of course, we can create merit and great reservoirs of positive energy through the practice of meditation—regular meditation, faithful meditation, consistent meditation.

I had an interesting thought during the last retreat. I do not know how true it is, but I would like to share it with you. I realized how wonderful and beneficial it would be to your life if you were to meditate for at least one to twenty minutes every day or every other day or for even only once a week. And if you can extend that to over twenty minutes or more every day, or at least as much of every day as you can, then it is for the sake of all beings. So meditate up to twenty minutes for yourself, and if you meditate over twenty minutes and more, then that is for all beings. And if you already meditate for that long every day, then consider this: your morning meditation is for yourself and your evening meditation is for all beings. Or maybe if you are not yet to the point of daily meditation, then come to the weekly meditation group and meditate with us once a week—that is for yourself. And if you can meditate outside of meditation group at home, that will be for all beings.

This attitude of meditating for all beings creates great 'merit' and creates reservoirs of positive energy that is going to come back to you and support you in your life and your practice. In Buddhism, traditionally we practice Dana, Sila, and Samadhi, and this means generosity, mindful ethical living, and meditation—these together create great reservoirs of positive energy. And we need that so that we are not just struggling and getting by in our life and our practice.

Bowing Down In Honor

Even the practice of prostrations and bowing is foreign to us Americans, but it creates great merit, great reservoirs of positive energy. At home we can practice full prostrations. We are not bowing to an idol or to some external force; we are allowing our whole being to surrender to the universe for the sake of all beings. We do not bow for ourselves, but we definitely get the benefit for ourselves. We bow in honor of all beings—body, speech, and mind, fully present.

You know, there is a reason why Zen masters and other spiritually enlightened persons in the world can just simply say one word or do one action and students suddenly have a breakthrough experience. The reason they can do that is because of the great merit and reservoirs of positive energy they have cultivated for many, many years. Just one word, one look, one action can be full of great power. The same is true with us—one word, one hug, one smile can ripple across the universe.

Yes. We can!

Universal Awareness-Part One

November 8, 2009-Dallas, Texas

Awakening To The Real Truth

The Buddha once said that if you take a bowl of water, pour a cup of salt in the water and stir it up, the water becomes undrinkable. But if you take that same amount of salt in the cup and pour it into a big stream of water, stir it up and wade in it, you can still drink from that crystal clear stream of water. The amount of salt did not change, but the amount of water did. In comparison, the same amount of suffering can be taken in that context by someone who does not realize that their heart, their practice is vast, and they will believe that they are small and unable to handle all of the different ups and downs of life. But through practice we can all begin to awaken to the real truth that our heart is vast like the sky—infinite, free and spacious. That is our true nature. That is "Amitabha Infinite Light."

It is not that we go from small to great. It is that we awaken from the illusion—the delusion that we are only our small human self. It is time that we awaken to the reality that has always been there from the beginning of time. We are the whole universe; we are all of it and more. And when we realize that and awaken to that—whether it is just for a second, for twenty minutes, for a day, for a month, or for a year—we just allow that realization to keep growing ecause enlightenment is infinite, and it never ends. We allow that awakening to keep growing. Through time and space, together as a sangha or individually as a practitioner, that infinite vastness manifests in real tangible ways in the way we think, in the way we feel, in the way we speak, in the way we act, and in the way we relate with others in the world.

So in our practice, we are practicing to open our heart to all the wonderful joys of life. Joy is definitely a very important part of our practice. Because many of us are used to focusing on the negative only, we just are not aware of all the joys that are right here and now. So our practice, first of all, is to awaken to all of that joy.

Standing In Solidarity

But a second aspect of our practice is to know, to embrace, and to be in solidarity with all the pain in life as well. This means knowing we are strong enough to be with someone who is dying; we are strong enough to be with someone who is depressed. And it is knowing that we are strong enough to be in solidarity as a collective sangha to stand for justice and righteousness in this world, even if it means that we sacrifice certain things in our life to help all beings. We can even sacrifice our life for the sake of love because if we are awake we know that this one body does not contain all of who we are. Even if this particular body falls in the act of love and sacrifice, we still are present in these bodies and in this cosmic body—no birth, no death because we are never born, nor ever die. We are simply manifesting in more and more ways, moment by moment, breath by breath, and heartbeat by heartbeat.

And when we awaken to that truth deep within our whole being, not just in our head but with our whole being, then when fear comes along, we can handle it. Sadness, we can hold it. Anger, we can be with it until it transforms. Joy, we can celebrate it. Love, we can offer it. Peace, we can radiate it. That is how *infinite* this heart is, the heart of who we are, the heart of Amitabha. It is so great that it can hold all the joys and the pains of all beings, because we are all in this together in this project called 'human life.' We are all in this messy and glorious project, this perfectly imperfect project of how to take 'infinite light' and express it in form, in color, in sound, in taste, in texture, in human life, in animal life, in all of life. And at the deepest core of all we know, that despite all the craziness of life, it is worth it. The craziness of life is worth it because it is here that the 'infinite light' actually experiences deep compassion and deep wisdom, with many, many forms—together.

Please Call Me By My True Names, a poem by Thich Nhat Hahn encourages us to look deeply at everything and everyone and to know we are the rocks, insects, snakes, and people—even pirates, starving children and members of the politburo. He ends the poem by asking that we be called by our true names.

So please call me by my true names: Amitabha. ChiSing. Catherine. Paul. Susan. David. Amitabha. Please call me by my true names, so I can wake up and the door of my heart can be left open, the door of compassion. The door of Infinite Light, Infinite Love, Infinite Life.

Universal Awareness-Part Two

November 8, 2009-Dallas, Texas

For my talk tonight, I will just let myself channel a little bit; it is nice to do that sometimes. And now I want to talk about some practical things. So just let the 'human ChiSing' talk to you too, not just the 'Amitabha ChiSing.' Never think that your human self is inferior to your Amitabha Buddhist self; it is equally important and precious. It is all one package, and it has its place.

11-11-11

A few days from now on Wednesday, it will be November 11th, eleven-eleven. And two years from that date it will be eleven-eleven-eleven. Right? Or is it three years? No, it is two years from now. Yeah, so I love celebrating that day each year, but even more so now because of the time in history in which we find ourselves. I would like for each of you to make a dedication and commitment to practice in solidarity with me for forty days. And I am using the number forty because in our Western spiritual traditions it is significant. Moses went to the mountains for forty days; and Jesus went to the wilderness for forty days, and it actually takes about forty days to get really deep into a particular practice to help transform your habit energy. So it is 40 days from November 11th to the Winter Solstice on December 21st. And in this particular year Winter Solstice is exactly three years before the Winter Solstice of 2012. So what does all of this mean?

Time To Shine Your Light

There is currently a lot of hype on the internet, on the screen, and in books concerning these particular dates in time, and that is okay. Maybe it will help people be more curious about what is going on in history right now. But really, behind and beyond all the hype, it is not really about cosmic cataclysm or global destruction or the end of our civilization in an instant; it is not about that at all. It is actually a symbolic wake up call, a spiritual symbolic wake up call to say: "Hey! Everyone...Ummm...Hello? Knock, knock, anyone in there?" This is a very crucial time in history. There are so many species, endangered species that are going out of existence. Global warming is increasing, wars are increasing, economic turbulence is increasing, and human agitation is increasing with all the new technology—with this iPod and that iPhone and whatever else technology.

There seems to be so much going against us, trying to delude us, and trying to distract us. But this time in history is crucial; everything seems to be accelerating like a critical mass coming to a head. So it is now time for all who are mindful, all who are deeply in touch with their true nature to make a stand, to make a deeper commitment to let that light shine. It is not that other people do not have that light; it is just that it has been crusted over with a lot of societal lies and junk, and they do not know any better. So it is up to us to let our light shine, and when we do, it will allow others to remember that they too have lights of their own. They will say, "Oh! Oh, I have a light too! I can let it shine." And when their lights shine, they shine all across the world. And in the next few years I hope that somehow all the spiritual and mindful people in the world can start to make a turn upward and allow a movement to take place, a movement toward universal awareness, a movement toward compassion, a movement toward mindfulness and spirituality.

It is worth it that we are practicing right now, because we will be the ones to teach our children and their children to be the lights in the world. We will be the ones that people run to for refuge, and we can be there calm and safe, a light for all beings.

Are We The Next Buddha Of Love?

My hope is that we move history up towards a more global awakening, so we can all collectively remember that we are Amitabha, that we are Maitreya, a Buddha of Love. It is said that the next Buddha to come is Maitreya Buddha—Maitreya means friendship and love and kindness. Friendship and love is not a single person; friendship and love only happens in a relationship. And so that may be a clue that the next Buddha is not a single individual, but a sangha, a collective movement of people practicing wisdom and compassion together. We may indeed be the next Buddha of Love.

So I would like for each of you to make certain commitments in solidarity with me for a forty day period each November. I will give you some helpful practices that you can do for forty days, then see what happens in your life. You know it really is nice to do this because it is the time for Thanksgiving and Christmas and Hanukkah, a crazy materialistic time with people rushing around and buying things, along with all the family dramas. So for the next forty days, wouldn't it be nice to practice in such a way that you are going to be totally at peace with all of it? You can be a light expressing the true meaning of Christmas and Hanukkah. You can be the light of the world. You can be the light of the world for your family and friends, your neighborhoods, your schools, and your work.

Dedicate 40 Days

I encourage each one of us to deeply practice for forty days each November as we prepare symbolically to be a part of the movement towards global awakening. So whether or not that date has any special meaning does not really matter; let us just use it—use it to motivate ourselves to practice deeper. Just imagine, what if in just three years we can be fully enlightened? It is not impossible! Shakyamuni Buddha did it in six years, and he did not have much help. But we have so many resources today that I think maybe we can do it in just three years—become fully enlightened. Let's just try anyway, all right?

Thank you!

Action And Being-ness

May 22, 2010-Dallas, Texas

When we gather to meditate, our practice together is a historic moment, a foundation for the practice of many others to come. And whenever we work through our stuff towards understanding and transformation, many beings are also affected. Every aspect of our physical manifestation—body/mind—is connected to all aspects of others. So if you are a male, as you transform yourself it reverberates to all men everywhere throughout space and time. And if you are a woman, as you transform it ripples across the universe, so that womanhood is uplifted just a little bit more in consciousness. Whatever your nationality, or whether you are gay, straight, bisexual, or transgender, as you transform, then everyone in that same catagory is uplifted. And if you are of the human species, then all others of the human species will also be uplifted.

So as we practice through our difficulties and struggles, others with the same difficulties and struggles will be uplifted a bit more because we are willing to do the work. But also know that it does not matter whether we consider our practice to be good or not so good, or whether we consider our monkey minds to be calm or very wild. What really matters is that we are in this room practicing. And the fact that we are in this room practicing means that many other beings have done their practice to make this possible for us—all of your ancestors and all their hard work and all of our spiritual teachers continue to offer the practice generation after generation. It is because of them that we can sit in this room and enjoy the benefits of this practice, offering this practice to all beings.

Being And Doing, Pick The Middle Path

When we become distracted during meditation, as in when we are feeling a little cold—if we practice with it, accept it, embrace what is, and just practice mindfulness of the cold without hating it—then that uplifts the consciousness of the planet just a little bit more. And of course now that we are aware of the cold, we can take action from that awareness. We can ask someone to make it less cold or make it less cold ourselves. What a wonderful gift it is in each moment to be able to embrace and accept what is and then act from that acceptance; in the next moment we can take action and transform whatever needs to be transformed. Yet at the same time, if we resist reality all of the time, it is very difficult to take action from a place of wisdom, mindfulness, and loving- kindness. The foundation of transformative action and doing in the world is based on acceptance and embracing what is.

So remember that it is always the middle path. If we are only just into action, we will burn ourselves out. We may be so caught up into action that we are not actually coming from the best place of mindfulness, loving-kindness, or wisdom. But on the other hand, if we are just about letting things be and accepting what is, then we might feel like we are nothing more than a doormat, and that attitude is going to the other extreme of non-truth. The truth is the middle path; it is both doing and being. So our practice is to come back to that being-ness, come back to that present-ness, come back to acceptance, and fully embrace what is. And when we do that we find that there is so much more in reality than we realized. Because not only is there this situation, which might be pleasant or unpleasant, there is also this underlying reality that supports us and holds us in the difficulties and the pleasures of life. And from that place of safety and support, we understand and can take right action by cultivating the beauty of the moment, transforming that moment into something wonderful. So being and doing are always together.

2600 Years Ago

Throughout time 'who we really are' has been expressed in many diverse ways: different species, human civilizations, religions and cultures. And one of the beautiful streams in that history of human evolution was the seed planted, manifested and expressed through the Buddha and the creation of a Buddha field, a Buddha field of wisdom, loving- kindness and energy that is supportive to those beings who are able to access that field of energy. We can also call it metta or loving-kindness. Sometimes it is expressed through the compassion of feminine energy of Buddha also known as Quan Yin or Avalokiteshvara. In Tibetan Buddhism, the mantra "Om Mani Padme Hum" expresses the same thing as metta (loving-kindness), and Amitabha (Infinite Light). However we want to express it, it is the same reality; it is creating this Buddha field. And the neat thing is that millions of practitioners throughout the centuries have been adding to this Buddha field, making it larger and larger. It does not matter what physical location we are in, we are accessing the same reality in the past, present, future, and north, east, west, and south.

Accessing the Field

As we are accessing the field you can feel the support of all of those practitioners. We can feel the support of the many Buddhas and Bodhisattvas who are adding to this field of energy that is growing and growing and growing, with more and more portals of access. Each of us brings a unique gift to that field of energy, to that Sukkhavati—that Pure Land. It is like we are planting the seeds of beautiful gifts and unique ways of expressing Buddha nature in our part of the Pure Land in a field of happiness. And so it is easier for others to access that field of energy through us because as we access it, we are creating a literal field of energy right here and now.

So as we practice, know that we have the support of many beings, many Buddhas and Bodhisattvas. Be mindful of loving-kindness, mindful of Amitabha, and mindful of the heart of reality, our access point. As we practice we will realize a field of energy is channeling through us, our thoughts, and our words; our actions start to emanate from the field as little by little the Pure Land is expanding right here on earth. And that is really the point of our practice. The point of our practice is not to become individually enlightened. We practice and become enlightened here and now to become channels of that infinite reality, to transform our reality here and now on this earth.

Amitabha Support

Chant 'Amitabha' when you wake up; chant 'Amitabha' when you are about to eat a meal. And chant 'Amitabha' as you step by walking in the Pure Land of that beautiful Buddha field letting Amitabha's light channel through us in every step, in every breath. Be mindful of Amitabha, and someone else in another place in time and space is practicing in solidarity with you, giving you their practice energy. You can benefit from it all by being mindful of Amitabha. And when you practice with that support, you support so many others; that is just the reality.

Middle Path Dance

The middle path is always a dance. In your practice just stop beating yourself up and let yourself be supported. Be okay with the fact that you are not perfect in the practice, just let it be. But also in your practice, you really need to stop being so lazy and get off your butt and practice. It is kind of like that saying: "Don't just sit there, do something!"—but actually, it is more like saying, "Don't just do something, sit there!" That is the dance!

Imagine a teacher on the end of a pathway and someone who is blindfolded on the other end of the pathway, and there is a fire pit on the right and a torrent of flooding water on the left, and any step towards either way will mean instant death. And the teacher calls out, "Go a little bit to the left," and then he says, "Go a little bit to the right, go a little bit to the left, now right." Is the teacher contradicting him or herself? Well, is it about letting go and just accepting or is it about really putting forth diligent effort into the practice? Which one is it? Well, it depends. Sometimes we are going to the extreme and the spiritual teacher within will then say certain things to get back on the middle path. So there is no contradiction; there is no contradiction between self-power and other power. There is no contradiction relying on yourself and relying on the other power of the Buddhas; there is only the middle path.

Remember to practice the middle path with the awareness that you are supported and that you are called to support all beings through our practice.

Amitabha

Asking The True Questions

Sep 27, 2009-Dallas, Texas

Someone once asked me, "What goes on in your mind when you are meditating?"

So the next time I meditated, I paid attention. Here is what goes on:

"I'm feeling my breath, feeling the body. I hear a few noises here and there. Feeling my heart energy, Amitabha, Amitabha, Amitabha. Gratitude, just feeling gratitude. Shopping list. What am I going to eat after this? I am really hungry. Amitabha. Amitabha. I hope I come up with something to say, because everyone is like expecting me to say something. Amitabha. Amitabha."

On Practicing Meditation

Avoid questioning and wondering because we cannot read anyone else's mind. Avoid thinking you are the only one who cannot stop thinking. Avoid comparing yourself to anyone else who you think seems so peaceful, so quiet, and so joyful. If you actually really stop thinking, then that could mean that you are dead, so be happy that you are having thoughts. To stop all thinking is not the purpose of meditation. Now, if thinking suddenly ceases for long periods of time on its own, that is fine, but we do not try to make that happen, and it is not even what we are trying to do at all.

But what we are doing when we are practicing meditation is 'dis-identifying' with our thinking mind because most of the time we are so involved with it. We are 'dis-identifying' with the thinking mind and coming back to big minds, big heart, infinite, vast, clear sky, spacious awareness, and consciousness; and we just keep doing that over and over again. It becomes easier and easier to re-identify with big mind rather than with small, thinking mind. And eventually, we are identified—we are resting as big mind, and the clouds of small mind are just happening. The difference is we are no longer the cloud; we are the sky just letting the clouds come and go. *You see?* We are not destroying the clouds; we are just realizing that we are not the clouds. We are so much greater.

So, some things have helped me in my daily practice and, well let us just say, in my meditation practice itself. I start off with just breathing in and counting my breath: "breathing in-one, breathing out-one; breathing in-two, breathing out-two." If I count to ten and my mind wanders significantly in such a way that I completely forget that I was breathing or even counting, I just stop counting and come back to "breathing in-one, breathing out-one; breathing in-two, breathing out two." This is what I did ten years ago when I first started. This is a very traditional Chinese, Vietnamese, Japanese Zen practice, counting the breath to help you with concentration.

Eventually, I let go of counting to just feeling the breath, feeling the breath in and out, identifying in and out—*in and out*. Then later on I started using mantras like: "Flower fresh, mountain solid"; "Water reflecting, space free." These were the mantras given to me in our meditation community. Then I started to hear mantras in my own heart and practice, and they became much more powerful for me as I used them: "I am home"; "All is well." And along the way, I started to discover I had a major resonance with Amitabha, the Pure Land tradition of entrusting in the heart, surrendering to the Buddha completely, surrendering to the universe, to reality, and entrusting, just trusting that there is this great support for me.

I remember one time a couple of years ago, I was just meditating at home, and all of a sudden as I was breathing in and breathing out —*Amitabha, Amitabha*—there was this deep peace that just washed over me, and I really felt the power of Amitabha in that moment. And I realized that I did not even have to try to meditate. Meditation itself was a gift that was given to me by the universe, by Amitabha, by the Infinite Light of reality. Each breath I was taking was a gift; every cell in my body was working and functioning as a gift. My heart was beating as a gift, and even knowing about meditation, knowing about spirituality was a gift given to me.

So for me, meditation is not about trying to become enlightened. It is just simply sitting in the gift that has already been given. So as I sit, I am just sitting with the gift of breathing, the gift of living, the gift of being on the earth, the gift of practice, the gift of spiritual teachings that have been shared with me and the gift of peace in this moment.

Amitabha is There Even If You Are Not

And now whenever I skip a day of meditation, which I do once in a while, I no longer feel guilty about it. I just put my hands together at my heart, and I chant, "Amitabha, Amitabha, Amitabha, Amitabha, Amitabha...," just for a couple of minutes until I fall asleep, because I know that I am entrusting my heart to this gift of reality. Reality is not stingy as in: "Oh, you did not say thank you to me today." No, the nature of reality is constant generosity, and so our practice is just to receive this gift, and whether we acknowledge it or not, it is still given to us. In the moment we put our hands together at the heart and chant "Amitabha," it is enough.

The merit of others is then transferred to you; all of the merit of those who meditated for the day is transferred to you as if you meditated. And when you meditate more than your usual amount of time, then you offer that merit to others. And so someone else in the world is receiving the power of your meditation practice, even if they did not meditate that day. You see? This practice is about giving and receiving.

All spiritual beings in the universe know that not everyone is ready for everyday meditation, or twice a day meditation, or long hours of meditation every day. Not everyone is ready for that, and that is okay. But if you can just come back to the heart and trust yourself, then it is enough to carry you to the next level, and sooner or later, just on its own, your life will just want to meditate and practice, not only for yourself, but for others, to offer that merit for others.

ADD Types Can Meditate

I have a bit of an ADD personality type, so if I can meditate, anyone can. I just stay with my mantra: *Amitabha* mixed in with "I am home," or *Amitabha*, "I am home," or *Amitabha*, "All is well." Eventually you realize they all mean the same thing, and it does not really matter what mantra you use. It is the infinite heart of love that is at the core of reality. I just keep breathing, feeling my breath, chanting *Amitabha* with my heart, and if I start to think of something else and realize that I am completely lost in my thoughts, I take refuge and chant:

Buddham saranam gacchami, dharmam saranam gacchami, sangham saranam gacchami. Amitabha. Amitabha.

I go back to my breath and the mantra, and then every few minutes, I just go back to: "Buddham saranam gacchami, I take refuge in the Buddha, I take refuge in the dharma, I take refuge in the sangha…," and by doing that consciously, I can re-focus and come back to Amitabha.

You can practice that chant wherever you are, and even if you do not formally practice your twenty- minute sitting meditation, the power of the practice of others is still transferred to you, and you will radiate light. And in time you will share the desire to transfer that to others by meditating every day.

And if you find it difficult to engage in meditation practice, then just come to the entrusting practice and also look at your ethical life. Bring mindfulness to the way you act and behave in the world towards others; be generous with your time, energy, and money, especially giving to those who do good in the world. If you do that, you will notice that your meditation practice becomes easier. Why? In traditional Buddhist teachings, before engaging in intense meditation, it was always recommended to practice 'shila' and 'dana' before practicing. 'Shila' means ethical conduct, being mindful about how you are seeking and acting and thinking; and 'dana' means generosity, giving loving time, energy, and material resources to those in need as well as those who are serving others.

Keep doing that and come to sangha every week. If you only meditate once a week with the sangha and practice ethical mindfulness as well as generous giving, then sooner or later you will see the merits of others. Amitabha will then permeate your being and make it easier for you to practice meditation, and not out of a sense of guilt or wanting to get something, but just in the sense of relaxing into just wanting to rest in the generosity of the universe and to say thank you. That is how I actually practice now. I no longer try to get anything anymore; I am just sitting as my way of saying thank you to life for giving me breath, giving me a body, and giving me life. I just sit for twenty minutes to an hour to receive the beauty of the universe.

If you meditate to ask questions and find answers through the practice of meditation, then in time true questions will arise from the heart, the great questions and the true questions. And when the true questions arise from the heart, the universe already has the answers, and because of your practice, you can actually hear the answers and practice them.

Amitabha.

The Greatest Happiness

June 28, 2009-Dallas, Texas

The lake looked at the mountain and thought: "Oh fortunate mountain rising so high while I must lie so low, you look far out across the world and take part in many interesting happenings while I can only lie still. How I wish I were a mountain."

The mountain looked at the lake and thought: "Oh fortunate lake lying so close to the warm-breasted earth while I loom here craggy, cold and uncomfortable; you are always so peaceful while I am constantly battling howling storms and the blazing sun. How I wish I were a lake." All the time, quietly, the mountain was coming down in silver streams to run into the lake, and the lake was rising up as silver mists to fall as snow upon the mountain.

The grass always looks greener on the other side, doesn't it?

At different times throughout my life, I have had a few heroes. I remember one of my first heroes was Captain America; then it was the Lone Ranger, Superman, and Spiderman. But as I grew older my heroes were Jimmy Carter, Al Gore, and eventually Thich Nhat Hanh, Mother Theresa, and several others. To me these people were the mountain, and I was the lake.

As I began to practice in sanghas, I felt that some of my peers, my brothers and sisters, seemed to concentrate better than me. They seemed happier, more at peace with themselves, and I felt they understood complex ideas better than I did. Sometimes I had feelings of jealousy, and other times I felt great admiration and wished that I could be more like them. Now jealousy has a shadow side, but so does admiration if admiration prevents you from seeing your own worth, your own beauty and radiance.

The mountain wished it could be a lake; the lake wished it could be a mountain. Yet the mountain was coming down in silver streams to run into the lake, and the lake was rising as silver mist to fall as snow on the mountain. What we admire in others is actually something that is pointing to a beauty that is also in us, and what we are so fond of in ourselves is also in others, whether in potential or manifestation.

In my own practice I have been very judgmental and critical of myself, thinking that I had not been growing as fast or not gaining insight as fast as other people. But then I had a moment when I awakened to my true nature, and all those comparisons vanished. I had a deep realization, not just in my head, but in my whole being that there will never be anyone in the whole universe exactly like me. My way of showing up in the world is absolutely unique; this particular body-mind expression of Buddha nature is wondrously one of a kind. And that goes for every single one of us, every being in the universe. And so if that is true, then there is no place for comparison anymore, because you are the only you there is; you are the best you there is. And no matter how convoluted or dramatic your story seems to be as it unfolds, that is the beauty of who you are.

The Buddha Wasn't The Buddha In One Night

The Buddha's journey took him from a prince to a seeker to a meditator to an enlightened one, then to a compassionate teacher, and so forth. And if you believe in reincarnation, then his path began much earlier in the many lives before. But even if you do not believe in reincarnation, we have past lives because all of our parents' lives and our cultures and the evolution of our planet have all happened to make this life possible. If there was even one moment or day or month or year missing from the Buddha's journey of enlightenment, then there would be no enlightenment. You see? You take that away, you chop it off, and there would be no way for him to journey forward on the path of enlightenment.

There may be days when we wish: "Oh, I just don't like my life right now. I don't like where I'm at right now. I don't like the way I am right now." On those days I encourage you to remember what I am saying today: "You are a beautiful being, radiant and unique, and those days are all part of the journey that makes you a Buddha." Do not wish away any of those days; do not break the path. For if any past lifetime had been taken away from the Buddha's journey—any day, month, year, even one moment—then his path would have been broken. Every event and each moment has added to the enriching manifestation of Siddhartha Gautama and his particular way of showing up as a Buddha, and you are also a Buddha on your path to Buddhahood. You are a baby Buddha on the path to becoming mature Buddha. Your path is beautiful, unique and special; it is your path. Maybe your path does not look exactly like Buddha's story, and that is okay. He is the only Buddha to look exactly like that. And you are the only Buddha to look exactly like that—your journey is the only journey to look exactly like that.

There's a wonderful sutra that expresses this beautiful truth so clearly:

> Late at night, a luminous being appeared whose light made the whole Jetta Grove Monastery shine radiantly. After paying respects to the Buddha, she asked him a question in the form of a poem. Many great beings and humans are eager to know, what are the greatest blessings which can bring about a peaceful and happy life? Please, Awakened One, will you teach us?

This is the Buddha's answer:

Not to be associated with the foolish ones, to live in the company of wise people, honoring those who are worth honoring—this is the greatest happiness. To live in a good environment, to have planted good seeds and to realize that you are on the right path—this is the greatest happiness. To have a chance to learn and grow, to be skillful in your profession or craft, practicing the precepts and loving speech—this is the greatest happiness. To be able to serve and support your parents, to cherish your own family, to have a vocation that brings you joy—this is the greatest happiness. To live honestly, generous and giving, to offer support to relatives and friends, living a life of blameless conduct—this is the greatest happiness. To avoid unwholesome actions not caught by addictions and to be diligent in doing good things—this is the greatest happiness. To be humble and polite in manner, to be grateful and content with a simple life, not missing the occasion to learn the dharma—this is the greatest happiness. To persevere and be open to change, to have regular contact with monks and nuns, and to fully participate in dharma discussions—this is the greatest happiness. To live diligently and attentively, to perceive the noble truths, and to realize nirvana—this is the greatest happiness. To live in the world with your heart undisturbed by the world, with all sorrows ended, dwelling in peace—this is the greatest happiness. For he or she who accomplishes this, unvanquished wherever she goes, always she is safe and happy, for happiness lives within oneself.

The Path To The Greatest Happiness

As I meditated on this sutra, I began to see that these stanzas were almost like someone's progression on the path, where you start by being around good people and avoiding foolishness and negative influences. That is a good beginning for some people. Then it goes on to mindful and kind living, and listening to the dharma, being with spiritual people, monks and nuns, and having dharma discussions. And of course, the path ends in nirvana, all sorrows ending and dwelling in peace

Every part of that path and every leg of that journey is the greatest happiness. So instead of rejecting it and saying, "I don't like this phase in my life. I wish I could be the mountain or the lake. I wish I could be in the future already. I wish I could be like that person. I wish I could already be a Buddha, a fully mature Buddha," you can just be right here and right now with whatever is in this moment, this phase, this lifetime, this body, this mind, and just do what is to be done in this phase.

And so maybe you are not ready for two hours of meditation each day, but maybe that is not what you are supposed to do in this particular phase. Maybe this particular phase is not to be around people that make you drink too much or do things that are harmful for you. And maybe it is for going to 12-step meetings, something that you are called to do; that might be your Buddha duty in this phase. Just do it; and do it with your whole heart, knowing that is enough for right now. If you can do that, that is the greatest happiness for that moment, just as much as the greatest happiness of when, sometime in the future, you realize perfect nirvana.

You see? This is the greatest happiness, right here, right now, to appreciate the beauty of this crazy looking body, the beauty of this warped kind of mind and the drama of this particular phase of your life.

Buddha, Jesus, And New Earth Spirituality

February 3, 2013-Ft. Worth, Texas, Harmony Fellowship

I would like to share with you a little bit about my life and my practice on the topic of Jesus, Buddha, and New Earth Spirituality:

I realized that what is going on in the world today is a major shift in consciousness, a really wonderful, new movement taking place among everyone in the world. Some of us are still a little 'sleepy' about it, and some are more awake to it, but there is a shift in consciousness happening. I believe one of the things happening is that there will be more and more people practicing more than one tradition at a time, more people practicing at least two major spiritual practices.

We all have two eyes, not just one eye. Right? Thank goodness we have two eyes that both see from slightly different angles. In reality each eye has a blind spot that we cannot see, but when both eyes are working together it cancels out the blind spot of the other, and I believe that is what is happening today. Some of us, like me, grew up in the Christian tradition, and I appreciate everything that is positive from the Christian tradition, especially the love of God as taught through Jesus and other wonderful teachers. It is a wonderful thing, and I would not want to give that up.

But at the same time, I have learned so much from Thich Nhat Hanh about Buddhist meditation and mindfulness and enlightenment and spirituality, and that is something I would not want to give up either.

Having both traditions working in my life in varying degrees has helped me cancel out the blind spots of both traditions and develop a greater understanding and vision that transcends both traditions. It is what I call a "New Earth Spirituality."

The art of flower arranging was developed from Chinese philosophy, and in Japan they call it Ikebana. There are three principals in this philosophy: "Heaven, Earth, and Humanity."

When we look at it from that perspective, the part of the plant pointing up to the sky represents the principle of heaven; the leaves below represent the principle of earth; and all of the wonderful flowers in the middle represent the principle of humanity. In Chinese philosophy the harmony of life comes when "Heaven," "Earth," and "Humanity" are all working together—flowing together rather than in resistance to each other.

> Brother ChiSing SIDE BAR:
>
> There is a story in Zen Buddhism about how the Buddha was going to give a very important talk to all of his students, and everyone was eagerly waiting. They said, "Okay the Buddha is going to give a very important talk, one of his most important talks!" But, instead he just held up a flower, and that is all he did for several minutes. The students all wondered, "Okay, when is he going to say something?" And then someone in the back, a monk named Mahākāśyapa smiled, and the Buddha smiled and said, "Ah, Mahākāśyapa, he understands." So what is the meaning of this story? It is that there is a truth that is transmitted mind-to-mind, heart-to-heart, spirit-to-spirit—beyond just human words.

The principle of "Heaven, Earth and Humanity" applies to these major religions that developed in China: Buddhism that represents the transcendent vision; Confucianism that represents human relationships, order, proper etiquette, custom, and ritual; and Taoism that represents being in touch with the Earth and the 'flow of the way of all things' in the Universe. But you can apply this principle to other traditions as well.

In the Christian tradition, you may think of the *heaven* aspect as referring to the Divine as God the Father or Mother, and the *humanity* aspect as the heart aspect of the logos or the Word, which was incarnate in Jesus who is full of the Christ Consciousness. Then the lower *earth* aspect is the Holy Spirit in touch with uniting all of us as one; the spirit of the Earth and the spirit of the Universe helping to unite everything together.

In Buddhism you can also see these represented in different ways. For example, in Mahayana Buddhism, we think of the Buddha as having three aspects or three bodies. The Dharmakāya is the aspect of Buddha that is the Buddha-nature which is transcendent and universal. The Sambhogakāya is the aspect of Buddha's manifest body (body of bliss) as seen in celestial visions, as in when you have a vision of the Buddha, and you might see the Buddha full of infinite light. Then you have the aspect of the earthly incarnate Buddha who came 2,600 years ago, Siddhārtha Gautama the Shakyamuni Buddha in his physical form. I am sure you can find these examples in other traditions of Judaism, Islam, Hinduism, and Native American spirituality.

In my life and in our current situation in America, I can see three kinds of spiritualities that will be very important in this "New Earth Vision" we are creating together. That does not necessarily mean that it is confined to three different traditions, but I am just going to give you three different traditions that are personally meaningful to me.

Personally for me, Buddhism represents the *heaven* aspect, the upper chakras aspect of spirituality. Buddhism has helped me to transcend so much clutter in my life, so much confusion and ignorance, and so much suffering. It has provided me with great insight and wisdom.

Jesus and the Christ Consciousness and all that we learn from our wonderful Western traditions have really helped me be in touch with my heart, the *humanity* aspect of love, forgiveness, kindness and compassion. Jesus helps me to get in touch with my heart.

The lower chakras represented in past traditions and current movements help me to get in touch with the importance of the *Earth* aspect. Sometimes we get so caught up in wisdom and love that we forget that wisdom and love have to happen in the body and on this Earth. We cannot destroy and pollute our planet while we also philosophize about enlightenment, saying that we want to love one another; that is a contradiction.

There is a book by Thich Nhat Hanh titled *The Sun My Heart,* and I love how it wonderfully expresses the oneness of all poetically—the whole universe, the whole of existence, the whole of heaven and

Earth, the whole of reality; the whole of humanity is my true self. Once we are able to live and act from that truth, then we will make a major difference in the world. Right now most people are operating from the delusion of wrong perception, thinking that they are a separate self and therefore acting out of that delusion. In other words they are doing everything that they can to protect 'this self,' even at the expense of 'other selves.'

I am not just talking about human-to-human relationships; I am also talking about human, animal, and planetary relationships. We humans act as if we have to accumulate more and more, consume more and more, and develop economically more and more. But at what expense? The whole planet is the expense right now—the whole planet! We cannot keep consuming and building, trying to uplift humanity at the expense of all the other species on the planet, because what we are really doing is destroying ourselves.

Love: The Bottom Line.

This is one insight into Buddhism that is a universal truth: the Buddha never saw things differently from other people. He referred to the foundation of Buddhism as the Noble Truths, and not because the truths themselves were noble, but because anyone of noble consciousness can see them. When we lift up our consciousness through meditation and through spiritual practice, we are going to see the same truth that the Buddha saw. The Buddha saw and understood our delusions, our delusions about the self, about suffering, about permanence and impermanence, and about reality itself.

The bottom line of Buddha's teachings is simply to help us transform our suffering by transforming our delusions; that is really the bottom line.

Jesus' teachings have a bottom line too. It is not discrimination, hatred, war, or self-righteousness. The bottom line of Jesus' teaching is simply love; it is even obvious to those who have a simple child-like heart that love is the bottom line. So let us encourage everyone who follows Jesus to practice love. Follow Jesus' bottom line: "Love." Love and measure everything else around it—love.

How Many Leaves In Your Hand?

Once the Buddha went to the forest with his students and picked up a handful of leaves from the ground. Pointing to all the leaves and the trees in the forest he asked, "Students, what is greater, the leaves in my hand or the leaves on all the trees in the forest?" And they said, "Teacher, of course all the leaves in the forest outnumber the leaves in your hand." The Buddha then said; "Well, the leaves in my hand are what I have taught you, and the leaves in the forest are all that I know. I have only taught you what you need to know to transform suffering and delusion."

So the Buddha knew a lot more than what he shared about the nature of reality. Maybe he knew a whole lot about the metaphysics of the whole universe. Who knows? But he did not share any of that, at least in human words. All he shared were the Four Noble Truths, the Eightfold Path, and everything else revolved around that. He shared the truth of suffering, the causes, and the cessation, and the path to the end of suffering.

Namaste.

Seeking, Finding, Preserving, Sharing

October 21, 2012-Dallas, Texas

The words seeking, finding, preserving, and sharing arose in my consciousness as I was meditating last week. A teaching arises from within me every few weeks, every few months, or every few years. The timing depends upon knowing just the right thing to do or say in a particular situation or just knowing about what truth I need to practice. Your practice is that way too.

Negative Aspects Of Seeking

Let us contemplate the negative aspects of seeking. What are the negative aspects of seeking? If we are constantly seeking then we only seek and never find. Seekers are always seeking, habitually putting off happiness while searching for future goals. Another negative aspect of seeking is that we can get so caught up with goals and hopes and dreams, unable to achieve happiness until and unless certain conditions are met. And yet when we finally arrive at those conditions, we still cannot enjoy the moment because we have now made a mental habit of not being present and not finding happiness here and now; we are still looking towards the future.

Take for example a coach who had just won a big game. When the newscaster asked him, "How do you feel right now? You just won the big game." The coach said, "Yeah. We are going to win next year, too." He was not even able to fully enjoy winning the game in that moment. He had already turned his mind toward planning for the future in the hopes of winning the next game, and that is where he was putting his happiness. He was not able to fully enjoy feeling happiness in that moment, right then and there; that is what happens when we are continually seeking. So be aware that if we are always seeking, we may not actually be able to enjoy the find because there is something inside us needing to seek further, putting off happiness for the future. That is something to be careful about—the negative aspect of seeking.

Negative Aspects Of Finding

So now what would be the negative aspect of finding? Well, for those of us who find ourselves just content with wherever we are in life, in our practice, or in our expression of enlightenment, the negative aspect of finding is that we are too lazily content with things as they are. We are without any motivation to keep growing, to keep expanding, to keep opening, to keep expressing the enlightenment that is naturally and inherently within us. When we are of the mindset that we have already found what we need, the negative aspect is that we are no longer open to anything else.

It is like walking up a ladder and reaching toward the highest value we can be; we are content with placing ourselves on the step that we feel is at the highest level. But if your foot stays on one step of the ladder and never goes to the next step, you actually never keep going to the top.

Many of my religious friends are content with their current views, and their minds and hearts are not open at all to the possibility that maybe there is more. There is more truth than what they have at this time; there is more truth to their own understanding.

The pilgrims who came to this country had this prayer: "May we understand God's will and word, and may we be able to bring forth more light from the word." They were open, at least theoretically, to having more light in their understanding of God's will and word. The United Church of Christ has a wonderful saying: "God is still speaking"—they say there are no periods, only commas after whatever God says. So, there is an openness for greater understanding and more insights. This is important, because without that we have only the negative aspect of finding and think, "Oh well, I have everything I need. I do not need anything or anyone else. I'm content with my little world."

Negative Aspects Of Preserving

If we look at the negative aspect of preserving from a religious point of view, then preserving can relate to the tendency to dogmatize the revelation as we have come to understand it, and then categorize it, systematize it, reify it, solidify it and close it off; we want to preserve it and cling to it. In other words, this is the only truth, and there is nothing else—no other truth. Someone once told me about a movie where many centuries ago monks were adamant about preserving the purity of the truth of their way just for themselves to the point of hiding scrolls so that no one else could discover them. So there is a negative aspect of this tendency to preserve if it means clinging and holding on to a particular way and understanding to keep it just for ourselves.

Negative Aspect Of Sharing

Could sharing have a negative aspect? Contemplate on this deeply, and we will find that everything has a shadow side as well as a light side. So a negative aspect of sharing would be to co-dependently give and give and give until we are completely burned out.

Giving in this manner promotes resentment and only leads to anger; it is an unhealthy way of sharing.

Many times when we give in that manner, we are actually creating a sort of busy-ness for ourselves because we do not want to look deep within. We do not want to face the fact that we have low self-esteem and have this inner belief that we are not good enough. So we do and do, give and give, share and share; we stay busy enough to distract ourselves from those feelings that gnaw at our heart and prevent us from doing the inner work we really need to do.

Positive Aspect Of Seeking

So what are the positive aspects of seeking? A very positive aspect is that it can help us seek for more light if we are in a depression. It can bring us out of our shell and out of our little hole if we get stuck. This is a very important aspect of seeking; but never become completely self-satisfied with that. We must always be open to more light, more progress, more openness, more expansion, more truth, or at least more understanding of the truth. So this is good if we can cultivate our seeking mind in a positive way.

Positive Aspects Of Finding

A positive aspect to finding is to find contentment here and now rather than to put it off for the future. We meditate not to get something out of the meditation, but we meditate to relax into what is here and now. We will find what is already good, right here and right now, finding the happiness that is already available now, if we can just be calm enough and still enough to recognize and receive it gratefully. So do not just meditate to get peace of mind or whatever else, but meditate and be with what is already available to us.

Oh, WOW! Now that I'm sitting here and breathing, I realize I am alive. I have breath. My heart is beating. My foot has fallen asleep, but thank goodness I have legs I can actually feel. And I'm surrounded by all these beautiful brothers and sisters practicing with me in a building that has been provided for my practice and that is available to me because of the generosity of all of those who have given money and time and effort and love to make this building possible.

Do not meditate just to get something. Meditate to be with what is right here and right now—find the happiness already here and now. If we do not practice and cultivate the ability to find happiness here and now, we will be too caught up in the seeking by putting happiness in the future; we will never arrive at it because of the habit of always putting it off, putting it off.

Positive Aspects Of Preserving

And what are the positive aspects of preserving? Well, when we actually find something worthwhile, cultivate it, preserve it, and appreciate it; help it to grow, help it to expand, and keep it going in our lives.

Last year when I was temporarily practicing as a monk in a monastery in California, I had several different revelations that occurred to me over a period of time. One of them was realizing the importance of having both conservative and liberal elements in some areas of life, and this insight also holds true for religion. I realized that, at least in religion, it is necessary to have both conservative and liberal elements present.

The conservative elements that tend to conserve and preserve things almost dogmatically throughout the centuries keep the practices and teachings of the past intact for all of us to access today. And the liberal element opens up these teachings and makes them available to the masses, relevant for all generations, suitable and adapted to the changing needs and different meanings of enlightenment for each generation. So we actually need both. And after that revelation, I no longer feel anger about the conservative factions and elements in history. Even now in our Buddhist traditions, I realize they have the job of preserving this tradition for future generations. And the liberals are also going to exist in every generation to make sure that what is preserved is not hidden in a container but is shared with others in a relevant, meaningful way. So preservation is positive and is actually good.

Positive Aspect Of Sharing

Do not seek and find something worth preserving in life just to keep, but seek and find to give it away, to share it. If there is something worthwhile, do not just keep it; always share it with others. This is very important, and in Buddhism this is called bodhichitta, the mind of enlightenment, the attitude of wanting all beings to be liberated along with you, the enlightened mind of loving-kindness and solidarity with all beings. Another translation is awakening heart, which is why our sangha is called Awakening Heart, to always remind us of bodhichitta, that enlightened desire to practice and become enlightened along with all beings, being liberated with all beings and not just for ourselves alone.

So I encourage you to practice the positive aspects of seeking, finding, preserving, and sharing.

Amitabha.

Shortcut To Peace And Happiness

November 20, 2011-Dallas, Texas

To begin my talk tonight, I would like to teach you a very ancient and beautiful chant popular in China, but instead of the Chinese version, we will do the original Sanskrit version. It is called the "Pure Land Rebirth Dharani." A dharani is a powerful, long mantra, and we can also call it the longer Amitabha mantra.

As with any mantra, a dharani has spiritual significance in the sounds that you are chanting. And there is a surface, literal meaning, but that surface, literal meaning is not the true power of the chant. The power is in the actual chanting and practice and sounding of it, allowing the vibrations to permeate your entire body and mind, your heart, and your whole being.

When we chant, we connect to all who have chanted before us, all who are chanting even now around the world. We are connecting to all of that energy, their energy and also the energy that has inspired this chant. We are connecting to that spiritual enlightened energy that channels this chant through all human beings for us to appreciate and enjoy:

Aum Namo Amitabhaya,
Tathagathaya Tadyatha,
Amrita Bhave,
Amrita Siddham Bhave,
Amrita Vikrante,
Amrita Vikranta,
Gamini Gagana,
Kirtakare Svaha.

This summer I was at a Chinese monastery where we did the Chinese version of this chant, and I had to memorize it. It was very hard in Chinese, but I learned it, and then I felt inspired to learn it in the original Sanskrit.

One of the forms of the Pure Land Buddhist tradition in Japan is called Shin or Jôdo Shinshû, or just Shin Buddhism, and has a very interesting and slightly different take on the interpretation and meaning of Amitabha and Pure Land. Instead of thinking that we are just chanting to gain merit and positive energy, trying to be reborn in a Pure Land and making sure that we are going to be on the path of enlightenment, just know that we are not the ones chanting; it is really the Buddha. Whenever we hear our voices say, "Namo Amitabha Buddhaya," or just simply *Amitabha,* it is really the Buddha who is calling out to us and using our voice to say the name 'Amitabha.'

Our chants are a gift from the enlightened ones; we just happen to be channeling it through our voice. It is really all about hearing, hearing the name and hearing this word that symbolizes the wisdom and compassion of all enlightened ones. And it is all about the support of the universe and all the brotherhood and sisterhood of humanity evolving together spiritually. You are just relaxing, resting, and allowing the chants to come through your voice. And you are hearing the Infinite Light saying, "I love you"—that is another meaning of Amitabha. Infinite Light means Infinite Love that is saying: "I love you. You are loved. You are precious."

Hearing the Voice

"Amitabha." This is the same name that Jesus heard when he was baptized. He was practicing too, hearing and listening. That is really our practice. So when we practice, even though it seems as if we are doing, we are really *allowing*; we are really *receiving*. So listen and hear. And so also as Jesus had surrendered himself to the baptism when He listened and heard the voice say, "You are my beloved," it is what we all hear when we practice, as like a baptism in a spiritual sense.

When we allow mindfulness to wash away all of the crazy stress, worries, chaos, and ego-driven desires for things that we have co-created in this world, then we can just let the baptism of mindfulness wash through us and wash away all of the unnecessary stuff. We can become receptive and hear the 'voice.' And the 'voice' will say, "I love you," in that moment in time as it has always done throughout all eternity, past until now. It is the same beautiful message that has always been there. And now because we have let ourselves be washed in the practice of mindfulness, we can actually hear it and receive it.

One morning as I started chanting this Dharani, the Amitabha

Mantra, I suddenly experienced what felt like a breeze gently washing through me; I was at peace. And I let myself go into this reality that had given rise to such a joy in my heart realizing that I did not have to struggle to guarantee my enlightenment. It was not as in: "I had better meditate today or else." It was more like: "Oh, enlightenment is a gift, life is a gift, and the fact that I even know how to sit in a lotus posture to meditate is a gift!" The fact that I even learned about 'Amitabha' as a mantra is a gift; the fact that I can breathe in and breathe out is a gift. I just realized that everything is a gift, so there is nothing actually to worry about.

And in that moment, I knew that my enlightenment was guaranteed and assured. That pure, inner knowing showed me how needless it was to worry, to stress, to overcompensate, to try so hard to be worthy, and I just let it all melt away. But, that does not mean that I can stop practicing or meditating. I believe that when we chant, we help ourselves enter more deeply and get in touch more deeply with the Pure Land.

Pure Land Meaning Relates to Merit

Pure Land relates to the energy field of positive merit, of enlightenment. Every enlightened one radiates an energy field of positive merit. When practicing meditation and mindfulness, we practice doing all the wonderful things like good deeds, generosity, and loving-kindness; we wipe clean the negative karma that has accumulated, and we support the positive merit. In Buddhism it is called merit or positive energy.

Now, we really need positive merit in our lives, so we do a lot of these practices to accumulate it and to help us so that we are not always obstructing and self-sabotaging ourselves. Have you ever self-sabotaged yourself? You do all the good things and then sabotage it with something that negates it. But if you can create more positive energy and merit, you are less likely to self-sabotage yourself and will suffer less bad karmic consequences that obstruct you.

For instance, what did the Buddha do before he became enlightened? He practiced meditation. And why did he practice meditation? To become enlightened might be one reason he meditated. But what did the Buddha do after he was enlightened? Why did he still meditate until the day he passed on? He did not need to accumulate good merit for himself anymore. He did not need to meditate to become enlightened; he was already enlightened. Why did he keep meditating? Because he did it for you and me, for all of us, and for all beings. He no longer needed any merit for himself. Everything he did from then on, from his enlightenment forward is only for others, to help radiate the energy field, the Buddha field, that Pure Land all around him so that many beings can benefit from this practice.

So that is what all the Buddhas of the universe do. They do not need anything for themselves anymore, they are just offering it to all beings. And so what is our part? Our part is to stop stubbornly resisting their help. Our part is to consciously access all the positive merit that has accumulated in the universe from the enlightened ones and use it, instead of striving and struggling so hard to reinvent the wheel. The wheel has already been invented; the dharma wheel is already in motion. So you do not need to work so hard at reinventing the wheel. It is already there. Utilize it!

Now because we are baby Buddhas, when we practice we can accumulate positive merit for ourselves as well as simultaneously offer it to others. We do not have to wait to be fully enlightened to offer merit to others. You can start right now because you are already enlightenment at your core, and as you are expressed as a human being, you are a baby Buddha. And even if you are not a full Buddha yet, you are still a Buddha in the sense that you have your own little Pure Land too—your energy field, the love and light that radiates from your heart.

So you can offer your merit to others in every *in* breath and every *out* breath, in every mindful step, every time you sit, and every time you chant. I encourage you to practice chanting for yourself and to receive the merit that is already there from the Buddhas, and as you chant you will also offer your merit to others.

Did you know that in a way you never really need to create any merit for yourself? I mean, in reality, you do not have to create it for yourself because others have already created it for you; all you have to do is receive all the good merit that has been created for you. So when you practice, you are not really practicing for yourself; you are practicing for others. Every time you meditate, every time you chant, and every time you have a good spiritual practice, you are not really needing to do it to accumulate good for yourself because the good for you is already available for you from others, from the enlightened ones.

So your practice is really more about offering. Your real practice is giving and offering the merit to others without being afraid to give it away, feeling you might need it for yourself. When I first heard about merit in a Buddhist temple, I thought, "Oh I really need to do good and get merit." But at the end of the meditations and chanting, when we were told to "...offer all of your merit to so-and-so, so-and-so, and so-and-so," I thought to myself, "I don't want to give all of that away. I need some of it for myself."

At the time I did not understand the reality and truth that I did not need to hold on to any of the good merit that I was creating for myself because others had already given me their merit. So the good merit I was experiencing was because someone else had already given it to me. The Buddhas had given it to me; the universe had given it to me; life divine had been eternally giving itself to me. And so, why do I meditate and chant? Why do I do good spiritual deeds? It is not for myself; it so that I can offer it to others.

It is like what Jesus said: "Freely you have received, so freely give." See, Jesus was a Buddha. Freely you are receiving, so freely give. That is it. Giving and receiving is the core of reality. That is why we practice breath meditation—breathing in, receiving; breathing out, giving. Receiving and giving—it has always been there the whole time. Since you were born and until the day you die, the message is right there.

Keep practicing this dharani, and offer the positive energy to everyone around you and to all beings. Trust that you do not need to do any merit for yourself. Just receive the merit that has already been made for you with mindful stillness and with every mindful breath, every mindful step, and every mindful activity.

Meditate this week on all that you have received and all that you are receiving. Keep cultivating the ability to be grateful. Keep cultivating the ability to call to mind more effortlessly all that is good, all that is a gift in your life.

Cultivating Mindful Relationships

June 9, 2013-Dallas, Texas

Thank you, dear friends, for your practice. This month our theme is "Mindful Relationships" coinciding with the last few chapters of the book, *Training in Compassion: Zen Teachings on the Practice of Lojong* by Zen Master Norman Fischer that I hope will help with your practice.

We will explore our mindful relationship to ourselves, to others, to nature, to our planet, and to our cosmos, but also to spirit. In Buddhism, we refer to 'spirit' as the dharma body of reality, or Buddha nature; there are many ways to describe it. But for us in the Western hemisphere, I think the word spirit is a generic word that for some may mean God and for others mean ultimate reality or cosmic reality.

Tonight, I feel drawn to share some practices that have been helpful to me over the years in learning how to be mindful in cultivating mindful relationships.

Beginning Anew

Flower Watering:

One practice that has been very helpful to me is called 'Beginning Anew' and is based on the community of Thich Nhat Hanh. The first step is *flower watering*, when we see ourselves and those who we feel to be our enemies as flowers. This helps to diffuse some of the anger that occurs when we are having difficulties with someone. We need to remember that like ourselves, they are manifestations of this universe, manifestations of nature; and just like a flower needs sunshine and water, they too need care. Flowers can be fragile, but they can also be beautiful—in their fragility is their beauty. So if someone is suffering, if we are suffering, we need to *water the flower*, the flower needs to be nurtured.

This can be done in many different forms: as a meditation so you do not have to deal directly with the person, as a meditation for your own sake and your own peace of mind, or you can do this process with them in person. You might want to explain to them what the process is before you do it in person. My favorite way is to write a letter because you can take time to rewrite it before presenting it, and you will not need to be afraid of their reaction right away; they have time to just read the letter. So my favorite form is to write a letter of 'beginning anew.'

Here is how you do that: in the first part, you write about the other person and maybe about yourself too, if you like. If you do that just make sure you write more about the other person than yourself—*water their flower*. In other words say all the things that you like about them and why you really care about them if they are a friend. And if they are not your friend state that you respect them as a human being. Just make sure that you write several sentences or paragraphs on this part because it should be longer in order for it to be effective.

Beneficial Regrets:

The second part of 'Beginning Anew' is *beneficial regrets*, when we share how we feel in case we might have done something to cause or contribute to the situation. Do not jump right away to what you think they did to have caused the friction, but instead try and see how you might have contributed to it in any way. Maybe you did not clearly hear or understand what it was that they were doing or saying at the time. Maybe you did not handle the situation as peacefully as you would have liked. The reason why we call it *beneficial regret* is not to label anyone as a terrible person. You are not victimizing yourself nor are you victimizing the other person. It is more about coming from a place of peace and strength and just admitting that you may not have handled some things very well. This approach is a beneficial way of dealing with regret and is very different from wallowing in self-pity and self-deprecation.

It is important for the other person to know that you see good qualities in them and that you are also able to see your own faults. The other person is more willing to listen to what you have to say when you are not so angry and confrontational. If they see that you are not just blaming them, they are more willing to see some of their own faults in the situation.

Sharing Hurts:

The third part of 'Beginning Anew' is *sharing hurts*. This part should be shorter and to the point, not blaming or criticizing but specific on sharing what it was they did or said that seemed to trigger in you such a reaction of hurt. That way you are not blaming them, just sharing only the hurt that arose when this or that happened based on what was done or said.

Gaining Insight:

The fourth step of 'Beginning Anew' is *gaining insight*. Developed over the years it basically explores what it is about your past that triggers your reaction to the situation in the first place. By gaining an insight into your own reaction you can express to them why you were hurt by what they said or did, because this hurt did not just come from you and the other person in the situation, but it also comes from your past. This step helps the other person understand you better. What is the point of communicating with the other person? It is all about understanding not blaming. It is not about revenge; it is to minimize and end the suffering.

We have to remember what our real goal is in the heat of the moment. Our intent is not to feel better by venting and making the other person feel what we are feeling. That will not be helpful; it will not make things any better in the world nor will it contribute to your enlightenment or their enlightenment. So we must keep in mind that our intention is reconciliation, understanding, and happiness for both you and the other person and all people in the world.

Brother ChiSing's Fifth Step:

Now, I have created a *fifth step* to wrap it all up nicely and positively. So the last part is to share a positive intention of why you communicated with them about all of this in the first place. What was it that you really wanted out of this? You share the intention that if you are friends with them, you want to remain friends; you want to make sure that the friendship is honest and beneficial. And if they are not your friend, then maybe your positive intention is just that you want them to understand or that you want to understand what they are going through and why they did this so that this kind of suffering will not be created for others.

So this is how a wonderful five-step process was built and has evolved over time, and as we keep practicing it more steps will be developed. That is how the Three Refuges became the Four Noble Truths, which became the Eightfold Path, which became the Seven Factors of Enlightenment; it just grows.

The Naikan Practice

Now, another practice that has been very helpful to me is something from Japanese Pure Land Buddhism called 'Naikan' where you meditate on three questions for seven to ten days; the three questions involve contemplating on another person that you are dealing with. In Japanese culture it usually starts with the mother, but it can also be the father or any other important person in your life.

The first question is: "What has this person given to me positively?" In other words, "What positive benefit has my mother, for example, given to me?" And you meditate on that for a couple of days. The second question is: "What have I given back to this person?" Then ask yourself, "What have I positively given to my mother or this person?" And you meditate on that for a couple days. And then the third and last question is, "What suffering have I caused this person?" In Western culture we think there should be the fourth question, "What have they done to me?" No, instead meditate on, "What grief have I caused? What have I done that has not been helpful to this person?" You meditate on that for a few days.

This is called the 'meditation method of inquiry,' of deeply being with the question, being with and contemplating this reality. We do not use our analytical mind; we just breathe with it, sit with it, and we walk with it throughout the entire day in silence, maybe at a retreat center. And on the last couple of days you can wrap up with insights that arise from contemplating the questions. And if you have time, you can contemplate the next person that you want to reflect on.

Just remember every person is also a reflection of everyone in the universe, so it is not necessary for you to resolve every single conflict with every single person you have in your life. Many times if you can just resolve the conflict that you have with your mother, father, or any other person within yourself, then it also helps resolve other relationships you have with your spouse or partner because they are a symbol, an embodiment, and an expression of everyone in the world, just as you too are part of everyone and everyone is a part of you. Thich Nhat Hanh says in loving one person deeply, we practice loving all beings.

When we say 'countless beings we vow to free' at the end of our bodhisattva vows, we are freeing all beings by freeing one being. If you can deeply free the relationship you have with one being, then you free yourself deeply because we are all interconnected; we are not separate. When one person is liberated, it liberates everyone. That is why at the moment of enlightenment the Buddha said, "Ah, all beings, all mountains and rivers, all stars, all the earth and all the cosmos are liberated with me." In his moment of enlightenment, the Buddha realizes that there is no separation, there is enlightenment for all beings.

Rehabilitation Co-counseling

Another modality that was helpful for me before I encountered Buddhism is 'RC' or 'Rehabilitation Co-counseling.' This is a wonderful process where you sit with someone and each one equally shares five minutes or more on what is going on with you. The other person just listens, and then you in turn listen to that other person; you switch the roles. So one person takes the role of wisdom, of Buddha, of enlightenment, of love, and is that love for you as you express suffering—holding you in that love.

This kind of dialogue and role play helps you to be fully in touch with the darkness and the light that exists equally within you. When you do not identify with the light that you are, then you suffer and are stuck in your darkness. If you do not ever identify or get in touch with and embrace the darkness in you, then your light is superficial; your life is not real, because the true light embraces the darkness, all of it.

Nonviolent Communication

And lastly the other modality that has helped me is 'Nonviolent Communication.' If any of you have the opportunity to do this and get trained in that, please feel free to do a workshop here at the Center. 'Nonviolent Communication' can be very powerful in the way we talk and use our language, in the way we talk about our wants and our needs and our feelings. Many times we do not really know how to express our feelings; we do not know how to distinguish between our wants and our needs. Rather, when we make a request, it is not really a request, but a demand, a threat, or an ultimatum.

A Group Practice

I would like for us to practice a little bit with each other. I would like for us to pick a person to pair with and to practice, taking turns really listening to the other person. One person is the Buddha and listens to whatever the other person shares, maybe a suffering, a joy, a concern, or something that relates to the teaching, the practice of meditation, or whatever they like. One person listens for about 3 minutes, and then when I ring the bell the other person becomes the Buddha and will listen. So we will take turns being the Buddha for each other, just listening and holding the space of love for each other.

Thank you for your practice!

Just Be It

August 17, 2014-Dallas, Texas

There is a difference between intellectual knowledge and understanding, and the deep knowing of your own practice. Think about the top spiritual insights that have arisen from your experiential practice.

Is there a difference between experiential practice and attending a lecture or spiritual center that focuses primarily on beliefs? Spiritual centers are only minimally transformative in your life because beliefs are intellectual knowledge which help very little and do not affect a deep transformation, especially the kind that awakens you to full enlightenment.

So does that mean there is no place for that in our practice? *Of course not.* We are not just spirit and soul and heart; we are also mind and body. So we have all these different aspects of our being that need to be nurtured and that need to be cultivated; they all need attention.

I grew up in a tradition that I felt placed too much emphasize on belief, and I did not learn as much about meditation and practical prayer. The only kind of prayer I knew was the kind that seemed to perpetuate over and over again, the kind that you learned in kindergarten and that never evolved by the time you became an adult. If you only practice the same spiritual lessons that you learned in kindergarten, then you will not grow and mature in your spiritual practice. If all you know about prayer is to thank God for this food or 'rub a dub-dub, thank you for this grub' type of prayer or to beg God for things as if God is Santa Claus, then you might want to look at your understanding of prayer. It should have already evolved, deepened, and matured by now. But how can it if you are never taught how to deepen your prayer life?

Deepening Your Prayer Life

Meditation is a very deep form of prayer. So I am very happy that all of you are here because you are obviously ready to go deeper into your spiritual life with a deeper, richer, and more mature practice of prayer that is meditation. In meditation we are not begging God for things; instead, we are just being with God. And if the word God does not resonate with you, you can use different words, such as 'true nature,' 'universal reality,' or 'Buddha nature,'—if you will. But I like to use the word God because I feel that it helps transform people's understanding of what that word actually means. You see, I am not willing to let the fundamentalists take ownership of the word 'God.' So I am reclaiming that word for myself, transforming that word to point to that deep universal reality—that true nature, that Buddha nature. So do not think of prayer or meditation as just talking to God; it is not a one-way street.

Being With God And Being In God

When we are in prayer or meditation, we are 'being in God.' And if you go deep enough in your practice of 'being in God,' you may even glimpse a deep reality of 'being God.' But I am not going to say it too loudly because it freaks people out if they are not ready to understand what that means. *Being God?* How can you 'be God'? Well, if I say I am God, and you are listening to me from the ego point of view, it is blasphemous.

But if you are listening to me from your deepest true self, from the experience of knowing what I am talking about, then it is very different from the ego's understanding. I am not saying that my human self is the same as the infinite divine 'everything-ness' of the universe, then that would just be an inflated ego talking. But when you practice 'being with God and being in God', any separation between self and other, you and God, or any boundaries we artificially create in our minds will eventually melt away. And when they melt away, there is only God, there is only being. And if you want, there is only 'being God.' *You see?* But if the idea of 'being God' is too much out of your mental range of understanding, do not worry about it. You do not need to say the words "being God"; you can say "being" or just "God"—just being, just this.

So if you come from a spiritual practice that focuses on correct beliefs rather than deep experience, then you will probably have a problem with what I just said because you will want to philosophically analyze how it can be that a limited human being can experience itself as an infinite divine being. That just does not make any sense, and theologically it does not ring true for your tradition. However, I am not talking about correct belief here. I am talking about practice and experience and a deep, rich 'knowing-ness' that comes from the reality of this.

When you experience that infinite reality that we call God, there are really no words that can fully and adequately express that reality and truth of being. And that is why any language will come across as a little bit off when trying to use words to describe this experience. So do not get caught up in the words, but rather keep coming back to the experience, to the reality, to the 'knowing-ness,' and to the truth of 'being-ness.' That is what really matters.

The Two Parts of Enlightenment

The first part of enlightenment feels like you are trying to leave things behind, leave behind all the distractions of the world and all the delusions and thoughts of others as well as your own. You are trying to transcend all of the suffering and problems and ignorance, all of these emotional ups and downs. You are trying to transcend the world of form and chaos, to realize the infinite reality of who you really are beyond all this form. But that is only part one. Part two happens after you have reached your mountaintop experience (enlightenment) and come down from cloud nine, when you walk down the mountain to the valley and learn how to express the enlightenment in words and actions. So the second part is how you express this enlightenment in your job, in your relationships, in the way you think and speak and act in the world, and in how you serve others. So full enlightenment is always part one and part two.

Putting enlightenment into two parts implies linear time—first you have to get part one down, and then you do part two. This is actually just an illustration to help us look at enlightenment. In truth, enlightenment is beyond time; it is timeless. You are actually in each moment practicing both part one and part two. And even though you may not feel like you are fully enlightened right now, there is a part of you, the real part of you, which is always enlightened.

So you are always realizing the fullness of enlightenment while becoming enlightened, and at the same time you are already enlightenment learning to express itself in this moment, in this situation, in this circumstance, and in this relationship. Both are true—we are becoming Buddha, and we already are Buddha. We are realizing enlightenment, and we are enlightenment expressing itself. We are transcending the world, and we are engaging the world.

The universe allows us to be very creative and diverse in the way we travel this path; so for some people it is really helpful if we do it step-by-step, linearly. For others in a particular place in life, this step-by-step linear thing may not help, but moment by moment reality and realization and the oneness of practice and realization may be helpful for them. So for beginners, it is might be more helpful to practice with the kind of goal in mind of wanting to realize enlightenment, because maybe that is what you need to motivate yourself.

But for the rest of us who may have already been practicing for a while, stop trying to be enlightened—just stop it, and just be. Just be and realize that enlightenment is already taking care of everything. Enlightenment has manifested this whole universe, has brought about our ancestral spiritual teachers, and has inspired millions of practitioners to practice and share their teachings of enlightenment down through the centuries so that future generations including ours can have this practice. Enlightenment put the idea in my mind four years ago to be brave and listen to an idea that came to me while meditating to start the Dallas Meditation Center. And even though I had no idea how to do it with no money and no help, yet still I was told to do it. And just within three months, it became a reality, an amazing miracle. Enlightenment is what leads us through all difficulties and sufferings in life; it teaches us, involves us, transforms us, and helps us grow. Enlightenment is what has brought you to this place tonight.

Enlightenment All Along

So, why are you seeking enlightenment when enlightenment has been there all along? Just let go into it. Just breathe into it. Just be it. Allow it to flow into who you really are. So when you sit and practice meditation, let go of the feeling that you have to be somewhere else, that you need to be more peaceful, more open-hearted and wiser. Just let all of that go—enlightenment has been working on your behalf for millennia. Enlightenment is not going to give up on you now; enlightenment is conspiring for your good already. So when you practice meditation or any spiritual practice, do it with the attitude that it is already done; it is already a reality. And so just breathe in and breathe out in gratitude. Allow enlightenment—enlightenment of who you really are—to express itself as this breath, this mindful moment, this affirmation, this mantra, this chant: "I am safe. I am loved. I am free."

We come from God; we exist in God, and we are destined to be one with God. We come from enlightenment. We live and have our being in enlightenment. Our destiny is to be enlightened Buddhas and bodhisattvas of this universe. So there is only practice; there is nothing else. Everything is practice. See everything as your practice, not just meditation—but practice.

I Am Because You Are					Richard K. McNeill

Two Aspects Of Our Practice

March 22, 2007-Dallas, Texas

There are two aspects of our practice. One is to realize and to trust that we are already what we want to become. Doing this helps us to relax into the practice, into life, and into our true nature. If we are always condemning and judging ourselves, we might want to re-emphasize this first aspect of our practice.

The Christian tradition uses the word 'grace' to express this teaching. Christianity teaches us to have faith and trust in the grace of the Divine so that there is nothing that we can do to alter the fact that we are loved and embraced. In the Buddhist tradition it is expressed in the teaching that we already are what we want to become. Nothing can change that fact. We already are a Buddha; we already are enlightenment itself.

The second aspect of our practice, then, is to awaken to that truth through diligence, right effort, spiritual practice, mindfulness, and meditation. In the Christian tradition this teaching is expressed through discipleship, to follow the anointed one and live a life of holiness and love and wisdom and truth—not just simply believing, but acting on it. In the Buddhist tradition this is expressed through practice by being diligent in coming back to meditation and in keeping the mindfulness trainings of non-violence, generosity, and regular participation in Sangha to support each other; it is also expressed through sexual responsibility, mindful communication and parenting, and healthy consumption. Buddhism teaches us to express spirituality in concrete ways through our right action and right livelihood in the world.

So if we are the kind of person that is perhaps a little bit lazy and a little bit too carefree, then we might want to re-emphasize the second aspect of our practice and come back over and over again to the discipline of meditation, mindfulness training, Sangha, right action, right livelihood, right parenting, and spiritual education.

Imagine the Mind Not Controlling Us

Our practice has so many different layers, even if ultimately it is only one thing, one reality. And as we live out our human story that one relative reality is expressed through many layers and in many ways. Part of our practice is to reach a place of peace in our hearts through mindfulness and through breathing, coming back to the here and now.

That peace can bring a clarity to our decision making processes as well as to our planning processes. There is an aspect of our mind that is much deeper and wiser than the surface intellectual mind that likes to plan. So when we come back to that deeper mind, we will have more clarity and insight in our decision making process. When we come to rest in that identity of our greater true nature, then the planning mind will no longer be master over us, it will be our servant. We can still use our everyday mind, but now it is not controlling us. Rather it now has its rightful place in serving us—serving our true nature.

And deeper than the happiness and the peace that we may find through this practice, even deeper than that, is waking up to who we really are—not identifying with the small separate self, not even identifying with the happy separate self or the peaceful separate self, —waking up altogether from that identity and realizing our vast true nature that is one with all. But before we deeply come to that realization, we must first let go—let go of that unhappy, disjointed, frenetic self to the realization of the happy, peaceful, stable self. Then from that place we can let go of that self-identity altogether and realize the vastness of our true nature, Nirvana.

In truth, our practice is always about mindful parenting. We are our own mothers and fathers practicing spiritual parenting of our hearts, of our minds, of our bodies, of our lives, of our world. We are the father and mother of all things. We are the Buddha, caring for all beings.

Opening The Door

June 21, 2014-Dallas, Texas
Summer Solstice 2014, Day Of Mindfulness

It is always good to practice mindfulness in various forms on a regular basis—whether through movement or stillness, chanting or silence. Of course, to do them alone is great, but to do them with others can be very helpful. It generates a lot of positive energy that we can share with the whole world.

Opening the Door To Spiritual Lessons

Spiritual lessons in mindfulness practice help us realize the reality of impermanence while we are dealing with our own mortality and the mortality of those we love—there is no way of getting around it. Acknowledging impermanence in our lives opens the door for us to work on other spiritual lessons like acceptance and forgiveness, a lot of forgiveness, because we have to forgive the fact that there is even death at all.

And when we feel those things, we really need to forgive reality for the way it is. That can be hard; it is as if we have to forgive God. Then we have to forgive ourselves too when we look back and realize that there are so many things that we could have done differently in our lives. But what is done is done; we just have to accept it and forgive ourselves, and other people as well.

Spiritual Influence

I always thought I was supposed to have lots and lots of people in my life, and that I would affect lots and lots of people. I thought that knowing even 100 people to be in touch with would be nice, but the reality is that having a few people in a close circle is enough. I let go of the idea of having lots and lots of friends in my life; I accept and value having each friend that I do have. I look at my Facebook page and see that I have 1,500 'friends,' but I only really know about 100 of those; so maybe I influence a lot of people that I do not know.

I am learning to accept that I am not going to directly touch every single person on the planet, but no one really does. We touch the whole planet by touching our circle; the circle of our family and friends is our influence. That is really the only thing we need to focus on and trust that it will ripple across the rest of the planet.

And I wrestle with the spiritual questions of whether or not I am doing what I need to do on the planet. Did I get a C+ or a B-? Am I learning everything I need to learn? And then here is the other big question: If I am really staring my mortality in the face right now, have I done what I came here to do? Especially when we are younger, we still have big dreams, right? But even young people sometimes die. It is not always only old people that die; you can die at any age. So it makes me think: "Oh well, maybe I already did what I came here to do, and maybe I have already loved the people I was meant to love. And maybe the big dreams that I always wanted to create—well maybe they have already happened." So all kinds of spiritual lessons are created through facing our impermanence. It is a beautiful, wonderful opportunity for growth.

No Need Dwell On Regrets

There is a great mystery to our human minds. I learned through our spiritual practice that what really matters is staying present in the present moment. So one of the practices I recently shared was not to dwell so much on all the regrets. Do not dwell on the sadness of it, but look at everything in your life—all of the sad times and all the actions and inactions, and try to see if there is a blessing there. See the blessings in your whole past and be grateful; just practice gratitude. Because who does not have any regrets? Who does not experience sad times? Who does not feel like they did not do enough with their life? Everyone feels that way, so we are all equal in that regard; there is nothing to be afraid of or worried about. That means you do not need to feel a higher level of guilt than anyone else. Regret is just part of being human.

When you practice being present, notice the part of yourself that is always rushing toward the future or is always regretting and thinking of the past. Do you ever do that? When you are mad at someone from the past, do you just keep playing that conversation over and over again, even making up new conversations? That is such a waste of your time. They will never hear it; it is only in your head. It is a waste of your time because it takes you away from the fullness of this present moment. So do not allow yourself to get carried away by worrying about the future or regretting the past. Stay in the present. Enjoy the present. Appreciate the present.

If I spend my present moments constantly worrying about the future and whether or not I am going to die from this cancer or be in a lot of pain, or if I will become blind because the cancer is near my optic nerves, then I am losing each precious present moment. I have to continually remind myself not to dwell on that so much because I do not know what is going to happen; I really have no idea. So I do not want to waste my present moment on something I do not know anything about. Part of our practice is to just keep coming back to this precious present moment.

Because of what I have experienced through this spiritual practice, I personally believe that the world was taken care of before I was born, that the world is being taken care of while I am here, and that the world will be taken care of when I am no longer physically here. There is a greater power that takes care of all of us, and within the physical world there are cycles of birth and death, growth and decay, happiness and sadness, good times and hard times. This physical world is held within the spiritual realm where there is no death and no fear. There is no lack; there is only light and love and life.

I try to focus on that reality as I am going through this, and you can do that with anything in life; you do not need to be facing death directly. If you can remember that greater reality within which our being lives, then it takes the edge off the fear—it takes the edge off the worry, and it takes the edge off the uncertainty. It may not take it all completely away because we are human beings while we are here, and we are meant to feel these kinds of feelings. So there is nothing wrong with feeling fear or grief or uncertainty, but those feelings are not the totality of us. There is also a part of us that is beyond human and is spiritual, and we should also connect with that reality so that the human part of us does not become overwhelmed.

'Earthing And Sunning'—A Heavenly Walk

A few weeks ago I was in Galveston walking on the beach with my shoes off, and my feet were at the edge of the water so that the water washed over them. The sun was shining overhead, and you could hear the seagulls and hear the crashing waves. And I thought about 'earthing and sunning'—a mindful practice. My feet were on the earth, on the sand, and in the water, and that is very good conductivity for the natural electricity of the planet to flow into my body; it is very healthy and healing. And of course the sun is very healing as long as you do not overdo it. So I was practicing walking meditation on the beach for 30 minutes, and I just felt this deep love and communion with the universe, with God, Buddha nature, or whatever you might call it. I was feeling a deep connection to the sun and the earth, heaven and the earth; and I was also feeling the connection of the breath, of the air, and the connection of the water.

In that moment there was earth, air, fire, and water all in one, and I felt like I was at the center of all of this beauty and love—my soul was at the center of it all. And I really felt this feeling of the harmony of heaven and earth and the elements with the soul, with my soul in communion with everything. Isn't that what we call God? Isn't that what we call Buddha? Isn't that what we call ultimate reality? You do not have to die to find ultimate reality; you do not have to die to find heaven. When you can practice being present in this harmony right here and right now in your soul, then that is heaven, right here and right now. And when you know and experience heaven right here and right now, then you do not need to be afraid of what is after death because heaven is always with you.

Wherever you go, that is where heaven is.

One Divine Nature Manifesting

January 13, 2013-Dallas, Texas

Thank you friends for sharing in our beautiful practice. As I was driving here an energy came over me that I wanted to share with you in our sangha tonight. It was all about 'Namo Amitabha' and "I am safe; I am loved; I am free."

Buddha-Nature

So there is only one Buddha-nature that manifests in many different ways. Historically, that one Buddha-nature manifested on earth 2600 years ago directly through Shakyamuni Buddha when he became fully awakened to his true nature. And through his words, his actions, his life, his teachings, and his energy, the wheel of the dharma was set into motion. We call it the Buddhadharma or Buddhism—the way of practice, of mindfulness, and enlightenment.

A few centuries later, as practitioners continued to practice and gain insight and wisdom, they encountered in the depths of their hearts and in realms of consciousness, the aspect of Buddha-nature as manifested through Amitabha Buddha—the Buddha of Infinite Light, Infinite Love, and Infinite Life.

And a few centuries after that, as practitioners continued to practice in their heart and in their consciousness, they became aware of the Bhaishajya-guru Buddha, the Medicine Buddha of Healing. Throughout the centuries, practitioners had become aware of many different qualities of the Buddha-nature, and they have expressed it artistically and metaphorically through these different Buddhas or bodhisattvas, enlightened teachers and enlightened beings. Yet, they are all simply expressions of one Buddha-nature.

But because practitioners are allowed to use their human creativity and imagination in diverse ways of practice, different communities based on their practice can devote themselves to expressions of the one Buddha-nature and manifest it in different ways.

In China, the three most common expressions of Buddha-nature have been historically Shakyamuni Buddha, our historical teacher;

Amitabha Buddha, the most popular expression of Buddha-nature; and medicine Buddha, Bhaishajya-guru Buddha, the Buddha of Healing.

In countries like Korea, Japan, Vietnam, and other countries, different temples and Buddhas or bodhisattvas symbolize the divine expressions for that country. For example, some people are very devoted to Avalokiteshvara, the Bodhisattva of Compassion; or Mañjuśrī, the Bodhisattva of Wisdom; or Samantabhadra, the Bodhisattva of Great Vows/Great Action.

But it is important to note that these three Bodhisattvas correspond to the same illuminating qualities of the Buddha-nature in Shakyamuni, Amitabha, and Bhaishajya-guru. Shakyamuni Buddha represents Wisdom, the teachings that set us on the path of enlightenment; Amitabha represents Infinite Love and Compassion; and Bhaishajya-guru, Medicine Buddha represents the power of our true nature to heal.

And this is present in all religions because there is only one divine, true reality. You can refer to it as God, Buddha-nature, universal reality, the Infinite, the Ultimate, that which cannot be spoken, the Tao that cannot be named, or whatever you want to call it. There is only one infinite universal reality, only one true nature that can be expressed and illustrated with different qualities and in many different ways.

The same applies to Christianity, Islam, Judaism, and Hinduism. In Judaism and Islam, there is a tendency to symbolize the Divine as the One, as Oneness. In Christianity there is the tendency to emphasize the One, the Divine reality in three modes, as in the Father, the Son, and the Holy Ghost; these three modes of expression are very similar to those expressed in Buddhism. And Hinduism uses a lot of different divine expressions in hundreds and thousands of ways.

Within Christianity itself, Catholicism and Orthodoxy both tend to express the Divine in differing iconic ways using many expressions, and Protestant Christianity tends to express the Divine in more simple ways.

But it does not really matter to the Divine, to the Buddhas, to the

Bodhisattvas, nor to our true nature, because our nature is 'One'; there is only one true nature. And if we feel that we want to express it metaphorically in a variety of ways to help us relate to the qualities of the One, then that is fine; it is all fine.

There is no need to create wars around it. There is no need to have jihads about it. There is no need for holy wars. We should have the freedom, as human beings, to relate to the one Divine in whatever way we wish. In all its unity, in all its diversity, in all its multiplicity, however we wish, it should be our freedom, our right as humans to relate in whatever way we choose.

"I am safe. I am loved. I am free." This mantra had come to me a few months ago during practice. Those affirmations are not any different from "Namo Amitabha" or from Medicine Buddha's mantra "Bhaishajya-guru," and it is not different from Shakyamuni's basic teachings on mindfulness. They are the same; they are just expressed in various, different forms. It is all one nature; it is all one dharma, and it is all one practice expressed in a variety of different ways. So whether you are practicing awareness of sensation and awareness of breath, whether you are simply practicing letting go and letting be, or whether you are practicing "Namo Amitabha" or practicing "I am safe; I am loved; I am free," it is all the same—it is one practice.

No matter what religious teachings we follow—Buddhist, Christian, Jewish, Muslim, Hindu, whatever works for us individually—we are all really practicing the same thing from different perspectives, from different angles, and with a different twist. There is only one true Nature. And we can call it whatever we wish but whatever names you call it, it is still only 'one Nature' and that 'one Nature' can have many qualities: qualities of the heart, qualities of wisdom, truth, understanding, knowledge, love, compassion, forgiveness, and also the qualities of power, action, vitality, and healing. And as you practice your heart will be open to all of these qualities that serve to energize.

Five Wasteful Energies

However, I have recognized five wasteful energies that can hinder our practice:

- When we tend to cling to things and cannot let go; we crave things and become obsessed with them.
- When we push things away, resisting things we do not like, feeling an aversion to them, feeling unhappy most of the time; we are never satisfied.
- When our minds are restless; we worry a lot, and that energy is going upward.
- When our energy is very sleepy; we are being lazy, slothful, kind of 'zoning out', and that energy is going in a downward movement.
- When we are spiraling in confusion and doubt, and we are not really sure what it is we are doing, why we are doing it, or if we are even doing it correctly; we are doubting our practice and even the teachings.

These can be hindrances on our path, but they are not problems; these are indicators for us to look for new ways to tweak our practice. One antidote to craving is simply to let go and get to a place of deep equanimity. The practice of letting go can help with craving.

An antidote to aversion is to accept and come to a place of acceptance and appreciation for what you do have. Gratitude and acceptance can help with that.

When you worry and are feeling restless, your body needs to channel that restless energy. So do something with your body like practice yoga, perhaps take a walk outside, or hug a tree. A helpful antidote is just to do something with your body to help calm that energy.

And then, if you are feeling lazy and your energy is sleepy and tired, a helpful practice can be to chant out loud so that the vibration creates energy or to practice bowing, an ancient practice offering yourself up to the Universe in gratitude and love. Chanting and bowing are antidotes that can energize your practice.

And when you experience doubt, confusion, and a lack of faith in yourself or in the enlightened ones, do not judge yourself or your practice; do not try so hard, but just bring yourself back to the simplicity of practice—it all comes back to breathing *in* and breathing *out*. And find one simple thing that you do well, just that one thing that instills self-confidence and faith in yourself; focus on that and appreciate yourself. And if you doubt your practice, go to a monastery and find someone more enlightened than you and spend time with them, or find others seeking enlightenment and go to sangha.

Come to sangha, and that will encourage you. You will find that there is power to this practice, to opening our heart to One True Nature.

Namo Amitabha

So, as we practice with the mantra "Namo Amitabha," we know that Namo, means to bow, to revere or to be grateful for, and Amitabha means 'The Buddha of Infinite Light.' But even deeper than the literal meaning, it really refers to our human nature and our divine nature. And the fact that they are spoken in the same breath, "Namo Amitabha," means that there is an intimacy there; a deep intimacy and interrelationship.

It is as if our Buddha-nature calls to us, "Namo," with a deep love, a deep compassion, a deep understanding, and a deep acceptance. Our Buddha-nature is calling to our human nature, "Namo" as in dear one, precious one. And when we say, "Amitabha," it is from the depth of our human frailty and vulnerability, our naked rawness calling out in faith and trust. We simply entrust ourselves to the infinite reality of our own true nature.

And so our human frailty and our divine reality are always in an intimate relationship, calling out and responding one to the other: "Namo?" "Amitabha", "Namo?" "Amitabha." And this is expressed beyond words with just the in breath and the out breath: Breathing in—"Namo?" Breathing out—"Amitabha." The whole universe breathes too, and this is expressed through the expansion and contraction of the universe: "Namo?" "Amitabha"—this intimacy always connects us to one another and to the universe. It is the intimate reality that has always existed between physical embodiment and infinite consciousness or spirit. It is the reality that connects the human and the divine and is artistically and metaphorically expressed in many ways and with many human words. And in the historical development of Buddhism, one way of expressing it is with the mantra "Namo Amitabha."

If we choose to use this mantra in our practice, it might add a light, a love, and a force field of support that we do not experience in our practice of mindfulness. In our practice we may not really need this mantra because we already have mindfulness, meditation, and enlightenment, but it can enhance it. It is like the icing on a cake, it may not be needed, but it enhances the flavor and appearance of the cake.

So as we practice basic mindfulness, add some 'icing' to your practice, add the sweetness of "Amitabha" or "Namo Amitabha" and maybe spice up your practice with "Medicine Buddha," or any other Sanskrit chant. It is good to have our basic mindfulness practice, our basic shamatha, our basic vipassana, and our basic path of dharma. But it is also good to sweeten and spice up our practice, add a little flavor and color to it, a force field of support, a bit of "Amitabha."

All those who have practiced before us have created a force field of support that passes along to us whenever we practice. We never practice alone. Just think about it and ask yourselves: "Do we practice alone?" No, we are always given extra support from those who practiced before us; we never practice alone.

We know this because the fact that we even know about meditation means that it has been passed down to us from others who have practiced before us. It is like everything else that we experience in modern life—cars, electricity, heat, computers, and so on—all these things that we would not have if others had not thought of them, invented them, and then passed them down to us.

So we exist in a force field, a network of the creative endeavors of others who have been here before us on a physical level and on a spiritual level. When we say Pure Land, it is just a metaphor pointing to the force field of spiritual energy that others have created through their practice. We are practicing now because of that force field of energy that has been passed down to us. And as we practice, we are also adding to that force field of energy; that is really the meaning of Sangha or Pure Land. In Buddhism we say Buddhakshetra, which means buddha-field or field of enlightenment, and in Christianity, it is called the Kingdom of Heaven. It is called many different things in different religions.

But it is pointing to the same reality that we are co-creators, that we receive what has been created before us, and that we add to it through our own practice. We are creating the Pure Land on Earth; we are creating the Kingdom of Heaven on Earth. We are creating The Beloved Community as Martin Luther King Jr. once called it. It starts with those that have gone before us; it continues with us, and it goes on beyond us.

In my life I have experienced hindrances that have affected my practice, hindrances like doubt—doubt about myself and doubt about my practice. Yet, no matter what happens, there is still a Pure Land available, a force field and Buddha-field available. There is still this practice available, and there is still the Sangha available. All I have to do is just mindfully take a step, mindfully take a breath, and mindfully come back. So take a step, take a breath breathing in and breathing out; always come back to the practice. And lo and behold it is all still there; it has not left and gotten away.

The Kingdom of Heaven never goes away, nor does the Pure Land of the Buddha ever go away; it is we who go away. It is we who take vacations away from our reality. Yet reality itself never goes away, it is always there; so all of us are already Buddhas. But we only act like Buddhas part of the time because we take so many vacations away from our reality, from our Buddha-nature. Our Buddha-nature never takes a vacation from us; our reality is always there. And in our mind we may go off into a daydream, a fantasy world where we may think that we are separate, where we may think that we are lost, or where we may think that things have gone wrong. Yet, it is just a dream in our minds, because the reality is still there.

The reality is: "We are safe; we are loved; and we are free." The reality is 'Namo Amitabha.'

A Buddhist Hanukkah Reflection

December 9, 2012-Dallas, Texas

On "Karma, Dharma And Seva"

I remember the story of a predominantly non-Jewish neighborhood where one night a Jewish family had a rock thrown through their window for displaying a lit menorah. And for the next several nights all the non-Jewish households placed lit menorahs in their windows until the entire neighborhood had lit menorahs in solidarity with the Jewish family.

So how does the story of Hanukkah relate to what we are going to talk about tonight? Well, as the story goes, the Assyrian Greeks had taken over the city of Jerusalem and made the temple unfit for Jewish ritual use. And when the Jewish people finally took back the temple, they found that there was just enough olive oil for the sacred menorah in the temple to last for just one day. But miraculously the oil lasted for eight days—longer than was expected—which gave them enough time to make a new batch of olive oil for the sacred lights.

I like this story because it reminds me of the miraculous resources within us that are not realized. We may think that we have very little wisdom, strength, or energy, or we feel like we only have just enough. Yet many times through spiritual practice, we find that we actually have much more courage, wisdom, and strength than we realize.

As a child I loved watching "The Incredible Hulk" and seeing an ordinary man transform into a big green muscular guy. It was based on some true stories, not about people turning into green beings, but actual stories of people in crisis situations where maybe their loved one is in a car crash and pinned under the car; and in that moment they suddenly have the strength to lift up the car to save their loved one. This also points to the reality that we have more resources within us than we realize.

So how do we tap into those resources, and how do we replenish them?

In the Jewish tradition this resource is Mitzvah. In Buddhism we tap into it by practicing meditation, kindness, generosity, or anything else of spiritual value that creates an energy called merit.

In Buddhism there is no separation between beings, and even though there is individuality, there is *oneness* within the individuality. Enlightened beings no longer need to create merit for themselves because they are already fully enlightened; everything they do just spills over to all beings.

This means that when we practice, we practice not only for ourselves but also for others; and others are practicing for us as well. So even if you feel like you have not done enough to create enough merit for yourself, yet there it is, the extra grace needed in your life in that moment.

Seva Is Service

This idea of sharing merit is called many things in Buddhism. One word is "seva" meaning service, and one tradition in Buddhism that very much emphasizes this ideal of service is the bodhisattva ideal. A bodhisattva is a being like you and me who simply makes a true, solid, firm vow in their heart to become enlightened and to help all beings along the way. The attitude of a bodhisattva is not to become liberated into bliss alone, but rather the bodhisattva's motivation is full enlightenment that embraces all beings. And bodhicitta, the attitude of the bodhisattva, means the enlightened attitude of the heart and the mind, seeking enlightenment for the benefit of all beings.

Meaning Of Karma

In the past few weeks a lot of people have been asking me about karma, which I thought was interesting. Karma means action, and in general, we use it to mean not just action, but also the consequences of action or the fruits of action. And in some translations, it is translated as reward and retribution.

So when first learning about karma, we may feel that everything experienced in this moment is only because of things we did in the past in this life or in lives before this. And so sometimes, there is this feeling of helplessness. We do not know what we did in past lives, but here it is. We cannot change it because whether it is a reward or retribution, we are just experiencing the consequences for those past actions.

That feeling can be very heavy because you do not even remember what you did in your past lives. Yet here you are having to experience the retribution of those actions. It does not seem very logical or fair, and many times you feel guilt ridden, oppressed, and hopeless.

Sometimes we turn it against others and say, "Well, you are just experiencing the fruit of your karma." Throughout history, in certain cultures, there is the belief that those born with certain physical conditions or those born into a particular caste or financial situation deserve it.

The problem with this kind of understanding of karma is that it is only part of the picture. I firmly believe that in this physical universe the law of karma is very much alive and well, impartial and nondiscriminatory, and that it works just like the law of physics. There is nothing personal about it; there are always causes and consequences. Our lives are a manifestation of the law of karma, and we are living out the consequences of actions.

And Then There Is Dharma

The good news is that we are also living out the law of dharma. In other words, we are living out our mission to be here to learn certain lessons. So if you are going through a difficulty, it may be just the consequence of certain actions in your life, but it may also be that it is the perfect opportunity, the perfect kind of situation that you need to learn certain lessons of truth in your life.

You came into this life to learn, so maybe you were born into a particular situation; and part of it might be karmic, but you do not know for sure. It might just be that it is what you need to experience in order to learn lessons on how to forgive, how to overcome anger, or how to become strong. So, be of good cheer, but not just about karma. It might just be about what you need to learn or what you want to learn at some deep level.

If you are in a tough, difficult situation in your life right now, it is not only because it is a karmic punishment. It may be more about your dharma, and that this is just the perfect circumstance for you to learn. There are certain beings on the earth today where karma is the predominant law working in their lives and who are primarily living out the law of reward and retribution. But probably for most of you, it is more about your dharma, about the lessons you are learning. So, do not whine, complain, or feel guilty; just accept the lesson that is there—the sooner you learn it, the sooner you can change lessons.

Seva, Karma, Dharma Integrated

The truth is that we have all three at work in our lives. We are working on karma, we are learning dharma lessons, and we are here simply to be a light in this world. You may notice in certain stages of your life that it is more about your karma, or more about your dharma, or more about seva. Just live it out. *Live it out.* Create the merit of positive energy, purify your karma, and keep practicing the truth of your dharma. Let your light shine. Share your mitzvah. Share your seva—your service. Be the bodhisattva that you are in this world, fully enlightened for all beings. We are simply to be of service.

> *As the leaves fall from the trees, they become compost, which then becomes fertilizer, which then nourishes the new flowers of your garden in the circle of life. So, do not hate your compost. Just know that it is all part of one whole.*

Live a life where your merit increases and increases so that you always have a spiritual resource within you, even in an unexpected crisis—not just for yourself, but also for others. Because ultimately, we create all this wonderful merit so that when we are fully enlightened, we have an abundant, overflowing supply to offer everyone else.

Let your light shine just like those menorahs in all of those windows in that wonderful neighborhood of love. Let your light shine into every single household in every nation. Shalom.

The Secret Of Meditation

July 10, 2011-Dallas, Texas

Every morning and every night during my week-long monastic retreat at a Chinese Buddhist temple, we chanted in Chinese, and it was very difficult. Most of the Eastern Asian cultures are very strict which is fine; every culture is a little bit different. But I did not read the fine print before I went, and it was not a peaceful meditation retreat. It was a disciplined precepts retreat, training you to give you a taste of what it is like to be a monk in the Chinese Buddhist tradition. So very early every morning we woke up to the sound of a gong and had 30 seconds to get up. We only had up to 5 minutes to use the bathroom or shower, and then be ready to stand outside, in line and in the right order with all of the other fellow monks; and our robes had to be worn in the correct way. There were so many little details to remember throughout the day and not really much time for breaks. At mealtimes, you had to know when to have your palms together or when to have them down at your waist, when to bow and which bowls to use for each kind of food, and then how to put them all back at the right location without dropping your chopsticks.

We were asked to memorize sutras and chants and were randomly picked to recite any time throughout the day and told: "Please recite the 'Whole Heart Sutra." Then we had to recite in front of hundreds, and it was sometimes embarrassing if it was not completely memorized. And if we did not get it right, after lunch we had to kneel for 20 minutes—just kneel on our cushions and stay there for 20 minutes to repent.

If I had known that it was this kind of retreat, I probably would not have signed up for it. But it was of no use for me to think those thoughts, because then I would not have been in the present moment. I know that not being in the present moment and dwelling outside the present moment creates agitations that lead to suffering. And that kind of retreat, where there are so many details to follow can be a real test on mindfulness. So I had a lot of chances to meditate, to repent, and to see where I had a need for more mindfulness.

And so, I was given a chance to experience this kind of retreat and see how thoughts really do cause suffering. Then, of course I reflected, "Okay. Well, I need to be in this retreat. I am here. So I might as well just be here now and accept it." Whatever reasons had brought me there, and maybe it was karma, I just needed to accept it.

But Then There Was The Snoring Roommate

My roommate snored like a bear, and the walls would shake every night for hours. I am probably exaggerating, but that was what my mind was saying. Then finally out of exhaustion, I would just suddenly fall asleep for like 5 minutes and then hear the sound to wake up. The first couple of nights, I had thoughts of irritation, irritation at my roommate and irritation at the sound of the bell. I thought, "Why do I have to wake up at 5:30 and get less than 8 hours of sleep?" And a monk gave me some advice: "You know, other sounds do not necessarily bother us when we sleep, like the sound of the rain or the sound of a bird or the sound of the wind, and even the sound of your own breath or your own snoring does not wake you up. So why are we allowing this other sound to do that?"

But on top of the snoring, in my mind I was adding something else that was making it harder for me to sleep—I was adding judgment. Because of the type retreat I was subconsciously sending myself this message: "I cannot sleep under these circumstances." And that was the affirmation I was saying to myself over and over and over again. And of course it came true.

So I followed the monk's advice and focused on other sounds like the sound of birds, the sound of rain, and the sound of the wind. And then I began to feel grateful—grateful that at least one of us was getting some sleep. And then I started to send these messages to myself:

"I am resting. I am refreshed. I may not be completely asleep right now, but I am getting enough rest and refreshment. I can just lie here and be still, even if I have to stare at the wall or ceiling or just close my eyes while I am awake and lying down. That is fine. It is okay."

A Sleep Deprived Meditation

Interestingly, just looking at it objectively, I was definitely becoming sleep deprived accumulatively every day. Yet by the last day, I did not feel sleep deprived at all even though I was getting only 4 hours or so of real sleep. I did not feel sleep deprived the way I did the first couple of days, and I realized it was my mind that was responsible for how I reacted and responded to the circumstances. Before, I was just blaming the circumstances 100%, but I came to realize that circumstances are only 10% of the issue; 90% of the issue was in my mind and affected my interpretation and reaction to it. So that was very, very good for me. It was all good.

Of course, now that the retreat is over, I am pretty sure that I will not be going to anything like that ever again. But if I had held on to that thought during the retreat, I would have just created more suffering for myself. Now after the fact, when I am no longer in the retreat, I can think that thought and make that decision; but while I was in it, I needed to be in it. Sometimes when you find yourself in a situation that you really do not want to be in, but you are in it—then be in it. Otherwise, you create more suffering.

A Nauseating Meditation Practice

A couple of years ago I was really nauseous with some sort of stomach flu, and I remembered something I had been taught; I tried to practice it while I was in that feeling of nausea and pain. I learned that just as I was feeling discomfort, so too was someone else in the world feeling the same thing, or maybe someone in the near future would be feeling something similar. And therefore, I knew to go through the discomfort in mindfulness so that I could relieve the suffering of others even just a little.

So by mindfully going through the suffering, I sent out a ray of light to people who were going through the same thing so that it would relieve their suffering. And if it did not relieve their physical suffering, at least my mindfulness might have given them some mental relief. Suddenly as I thought on that, even though I still had a little nausea and pain; I noticed it had lessened from 100% to 75%. I felt a noticeable difference in the pain. It went down because of this turn around in attitude. It will work in the same way even if you are sweating in the hot sun or doing anything difficult. You can use this as energy and send it out as a blessing to someone.

Meditation Preferences

Even though I prefer a gentler retreat and meditation practice, I am not necessarily criticizing the Chinese Buddhist way. In fact, it has given me an insight as to why it is the way it is. Things are just the way they are; we do not always know the reason, but they are. And there may be a reason for it now or in the future, but we do not necessarily see it. Things are as they are. And as I reflected on it, I realize traditions that are strict are very much like thick and impenetrable, hard containers that hold precious liquids or substances inside. The harder, more impenetrable and thicker the container, the more likely it will endure for several years, decades, centuries, and millennia.

You see, Chinese Buddhists today have a lot of giant temples with a lot of practitioners, and I realize that they are going to last for centuries. They are going to last a long time. And yes, I do believe they need a little bit of reform also and need to lighten up a bit. But it is okay that they are a little strict, because if they had not been strict for the last several centuries, they might not have been able to withstand all of the wars, emperors, and communist governments that tried to suppress Buddhism; they would not exist today.

So when the time comes for a great Buddhist teacher whom everyone respects to lighten the way, it will happen at the right time in the future. There is reform happening in Buddhism, and Thich Nhat Hanh is one of the prime examples of reformed Buddhism, humane Buddhism, real and engaged Buddhism. That is why I so appreciate him.

The Non-Secret Of Zen

June 26, 2011-Dallas, Texas

Tonight we will be talking about the secret of Zen. And as I meditated on this, I realized that the secret cannot be spoken. So, actually I will talk about three 'non-secrets': letting go, letting be, and letting flow.

1st Non-Secret Of Zen–Letting Go

When you practice, practice 'letting go'—the actual essence of practice is not about acquiring things. Although it is our tendency and especially in our Western culture, we seek to obtain enlightenment, happiness, and wisdom. And that kind of motivation is okay in the beginning of our practice because it is better to start with something rather than nothing—at least it gets us through the door and keeps us going. And that is fine; there is nothing wrong with that.

Over time we start to realize that it really is not about getting enlightenment or anything else. It is more about letting go—letting go of ignorance, letting go of delusion, letting go of attachment, letting go of aversion—letting go of all those different things that have accumulated around our hearts and keep us from allowing the light that is already there to shine fully.

All of us are like dirty light bulbs; we are already connected. The switch is on, and the light is already shining; but we cannot see it or feel it fully because there is so much muck around our bulb. So our practice is really not to get the light, because we already are the light. Our practice is to slowly let go, let go, let go of all the accumulations and dirt that prevents us from really realizing and embodying the bright lights that we are.

And there is no such thing as Buddhist light versus Christian light versus Jewish light versus Hindu light versus secular light; it is all light. If it helps you to have a Buddhist lampshade or a Christian lampshade, that is fine. Diversity is a part of life, and that is the light itself. There is no such thing as Buddhist light or Christian light—there is only one light.

So let go; let go; let go. And as you let go, you start to feel the fruits of letting go, feeling more at peace and more at home in the present moment: "I am home." "I am home." Keep practicing letting go with every breath. Sometimes we emphasize the in breath or maybe equally the in breath and the out breath, but in one particular teaching of Zen, the emphasis is really on the out breath, because we are 'letting go' with the out breath.

And if you can practice letting go with the out breath, you do not even need to worry about the in breath. Just let go, and let yourself completely surrender into the out breath. Let yourself completely go, surrendering into the infiniteness of the universe. Let all attachments go, and trust yourself; let go into the great unknown with every out breath.

Like A Gift Of Grace

As we let go, the in breath happens effortlessly without even trying, like a gift of grace. And as we feel the happiness and joy of the in breath, we are very grateful for this gift of grace; it is an automatic response. But we do not hold onto this gift—we still let it go.

That is the key, even in our daily life. When we receive gifts of grace, we just receive it with joy, and we celebrate it; and then instead of clinging to it, we also let it go. If we stifle the energy of any gift from the universe including the energy of money, we will suffocate ourselves, literally and metaphorically. Guess what? If you hold on to the in breath, it does not work. So as you receive these gifts do not cling—receive them and celebrate, but let go. Just let go with the out breath once again. The gift of life comes without even making it happen. It is a gift of grace.

And that is why meditation on the breath is so powerful, because if we truly meditate on the breath, we will have insights that help us. If we can be grateful for the breath, then it will not be so hard to be grateful for anything else. When we are grateful for something as simple and ordinary as the breath, then everything becomes extraordinary around us. So let go. Let go. Peace is natural. Feeling present is natural. 'I am home in the present moment' becomes natural.

2nd Non-Secret of Zen – Letting Be

The second non-secret of Zen is 'letting be.' Now, letting be has many different meanings. The one particular meaning I want to emphasize is letting be as in the sense of 'letting *Be*' with a capital *B*, and *Be* meaning being or being-ness. This is the insight of enlightenment.

The insight of letting go is where we start. We start with the practice of letting go, and then we will uncover the gift of being present in the here and now, being at peace and having a smoother, more stress free life—just letting the light shine. And as we keep practicing and deepening in the practice, there will suddenly be an opening. In Buddhism, we call it different things; one particular word is kensho in the Japanese Zen tradition, which means to see our true nature.

There is only 'one' true nature. It is not like my nature or your nature or his nature or her nature. We are all manifestations of one nature that we see, and I do not literally mean that we physically see it, but it does include that. It is to see, to perceive, to really be it, that is what we mean, to fully embody it and feel it with our whole being. And so that is what I mean by letting be—seeing your true being-ness, to see being with our whole being.

And that is another meaning of "I am home"—I am Home with a capital *H* meaning not just 'I am at home in the here and the now' or 'I'm getting to be at home with peace and love and joy,' but actually realizing that I am the home that I've been seeking all along, that I am one with the great infinite home, and I have always been home. I have never left; I only fell asleep and dreamt that I left, but I have never left. I have always been home here. I have always been the 'Great I Am'. I have always been Buddha nature; I just fell asleep and forgot for a little while. But even as I fell asleep and forgot, I was sleeping in the bed of Buddha, in the bed of the divine, in the bed of heaven.

3rd Non-Secret Of Zen – Letting Flow

And last, but not least—the 3rd non-secret of Zen is 'letting flow.' To become fully enlightened we not only let go and let be, which we need, but we also let flow. I want to emphasize tonight that it is not all about finding peace in each moment, which in itself is wonderful—but that is not all. When finding enlightenment, we practice enlightenment.

For our enlightenment to be full enlightenment we let go, we let be, and we let flow. What do I mean by letting flow? Letting flow has many different meanings. Letting flow means allowing the realization of enlightenment to become embodied in our minds, affecting every emotional, psychological, social, and physical aspect of our lives. Letting flow affects every relationship and transforms all areas of our lives as individuals, as families, as communities, as nations, as a whole planet.

The enlightenment of realizing who you truly are is not the end of enlightenment; it is only half of enlightenment. So make sure you do not get stuck in your half enlightenment; you still need to grow. There are still things you need to learn. It is like being a sophomore when you finally know everything and are way smarter than freshmen, but there are still other things to be learned from which to grow.

So let it flow means that *I*, meaning the individual *I*, have now realized the great 'I' is in harmony creating and co-creating a life, a Pure Land, a heaven on earth as a home for all beings. I co-create home for others so that all beings feel and know home, refuge, safety, love, family, because of me and all my brothers and sisters together. And that is the true meaning of 'I am home.'

Our true nature's mission is to awaken first to who we always have been and who we always will be. And once we awaken to that, then we manifest new and creative ways to forever make this universe a friendly, welcoming home for all baby Buddhas so that we can keep going forever.

You see, in one sense enlightenment is a once and for all awakening, but in another sense, enlightenment never ends and continues on forever because there are always new and creative ways to express enlightenment in the physical world through our words and our actions.

For instance, Buddha did not have iPods or CD players or any of the things we have today, but there are so many new ways that we can express the truth. So if silent meditation is kind of hard for you right now, that is okay. You can listen to a guided meditation or chanting music to help you meditate until you get to the point when you do not need it anymore and can meditate silently.

You can also use meditation beads to help you. I still use them from time to time when my crazy ADD mind is really active. I breathe with each bead: *Namo Amitabha, Namo Amitabha, Namo Amitabha*. I go to each bead until I get to the main bead, and one round of beads is about 12 minutes for me; so I know that one round is 12 minutes, and two rounds is 24 minutes of meditation. And that helps me stay grounded physically in my body, in the present moment, and in the here and now, because I have a tendency to go off into fantasyland.

We are all baby Buddhas. None of us have graduated, or we would not be here. Just do what you need to do. There is no comparison. Not every Buddha is going to be like your Buddha; every Buddha will be different. There are no Buddhas in the whole universe of infinite Buddhas that are exactly alike; there is no one to compare yourself with. You have no one to judge and no one to judge you. You are very unique and beautiful, and if you do not know it yet, it is okay. Other people will know it for you. I know it for you, and when I see you, I see how beautiful you are. And my hope is that someday you will see how beautiful you are too.

Amitabha.

Honoring The Clouds Of Our Practice
August 22, 2010-Dallas, Texas

In Buddhism, we honor clouds a lot. For instance, there is the Compassionate Dharma Cloud Monastery, Clouds in Water Zen Center in St. Paul, and Auspicious Clouds. And clouds have different meanings like the clouds of dharma that just kind of waft through and pervade everything or like the clouds that disturb our thoughts just going in and out. But in Buddhism, we do not hate things that disturb us. In fact, we honor them and use them in names for our monasteries and Zen centers.

It is the same with our monkey mind. Even though it sometimes drives us crazy, we do not hate it; we honor it. We have a beautiful place for the monkey mind in our practice. It is always sitting back and watching all of us, as are the clouds above us. Yes, our thoughts are going in and out, but those thoughts and the monkey mind are actually the same thing. Because even though they seem disturbing from the unenlightened perspective and cannot be seen, from an enlightened perspective the monkey mind and clouds actually stem from that deep place within us, which is the source of creativity, creative thinking, and new ideas. So we do not hate them; we just incorporate them and include them in a mindful way.

Deepening Your Practice With QiGong

I noticed after four days of intensive QiGong practice at a retreat in Austin this past week how sensitive I had become to the energy around me.

QiGong is so simple, and yet at the same time can be so powerful—just like sitting and meditating for 20 minutes. If we were to incorporate QiGong into our practice and our lives, I believe that it would have a profound effect on our meditation practices and our life, deepening and transforming our experience.

It is the same for yoga practice. I did a yoga class a week after a conference, and I could feel the power of the prana energy. And then whenever I encountered someone of a high vibration, my hands would tingle. But when I spent time with someone who had a very low vibration, I noticed a yucky feeling, and it was very, very stark. And now I notice every time I chant "Namo Amitabha Buddhaya," 10 times during the 10 periods of the day, I think, "Wow!" I can feel the vibration of all the people who are practicing with me, and my hands just vibrate and tingle. It is very, very beautiful and is so wonderful, a very nice experience. For weeks after that conference, I was still so sensitive to energy.

Another benefit to the energy work was that my meditations, instead of being difficult, were just so effortless. I was actually surprised when I opened my eyes, saw the timer, and noticed that 30 minutes had passed—I thought it had only been five minutes. I highly recommend that you practice QiGong or yoga or some other kind of subtle energy movement modality that cleanses and rejuvenates your body energy, freeing it and making it vibrant. Your meditation will be deeper, and your life will be deeper.

Practicing Under A Very Dark Cloud

Yesterday one of our attendees suddenly had a convulsion in the middle of our meditation workshop. I did not know w chat to do. Just imagine that you are in a silent and peaceful meditation and someone starts convulsing; it was a scary situation.

I decided to hold him, and we were all surrounding him with loving-kindness. We were just giving him loving-kindness, Amitabha light energy, and praying for him. And a part of me was thinking: "I have never had anyone die in my arms before. Will I be able to handle this? And what about everyone else? Will they be able to handle this?" I did not know what was going to happen, but I did know that I was completely there to experience whatever unfolded because I was not in control. This was not about me; this was about him. And this was his moment and our moment together; I was just witnessing and allowing. And that was what we have to do, especially in crisis situations, to witness and to allow.

If we had been frantically running around, we would not have been able to help him and might have made him worse. So our peacefulness, our quietness, our attention, and our loving-kindness was very helpful.

After that situation, I asked Buddha; "What am I going to do to complete the meditation? What is going to be in that room with all of these people in shock? What am I going to do?" But the moment I walked back into the room, I saw about 16 women holding hands in silent prayer; I was stunned by the image and felt a powerful, strong Goddess energy. And I thought to myself, "I don't even need to teach them anything. They are just pretending they need to learn something, and I guess I will just go along with that."

We finished the workshop powerfully, beautifully, and mindfully with such strength, such deep heartfelt tears. We all learned from our shared experience yesterday by not rejecting it, but by opening our hearts to that whole experience.

I visited him in the hospital later that day, and he looked completely fine. He was awake and did not remember anything that had happened. I think all of our healing energy really was with him deeply, and there was nothing else wrong with him other than he might have had a seizure. I felt all of this was divine order unfolding when I noticed that everyone except him had signed the registration page for the retreat in black ink; he had used blue ink. It was as if something was bound to happen that day, and it was all going to be part of the retreat, part of the learning experience, part of the growth and transformation. And as I walked into the hospital, I ran into a friend that I had not seen in 10 years. And that was very interesting because it just so happened that I had been having dreams about this friend for the last few months—another sign of synchronicity.

None Of That Matters

Yesterday's experience has also helped me with a recent situation. I had been receiving a few unpleasant e-mails and some mean looks from one particular person with whom I had a disagreement. I had felt that I was trying to do my best here and be a light in Dallas, so I did not understand the criticism of me; and it had really been bothering me. I just did not need any of that. But I realized after yesterday that none of that really matters. We are living life, and we are all on the borderline of life and death. What matters is living life fully and deeply, because you never know the moment you are going to transition. So be here now; you never know what tomorrow brings.

It was such a deep powerful teaching for me in my heart. Now it is a lot easier just to let go of those unpleasant texts, e-mails, and mean looks. I just tell myself, "Whatever!" That is the new mantra: "Whatever!" So use that this week—"whatever!" Come back to what is really important, what is really essential, and what really matters.

So, take a deep breath.
Amitabha.

Clouds In Water

Universal Peace

November 11, 2011-Dallas, Texas

In the 60's and 70's, and especially here in this country, there was a great movement toward the ideal of oneness, peace, brotherhood and sisterhood with the aid of songs and marches and even herbs. But somehow the momentum of that movement seems to have fizzled a little. It may have moved on to different areas, but it did not have the desired impact.

I think about that, and I wonder why that is. I think it is because there was a missing ingredient. Yes, it is important to have ideals; it is important to have dreams and to nurture our heart's truest desire for peace. But that by itself is not enough. There needs to be a spiritual practice giving those ideals power, momentum, and lasting force.

So, today on 11/11/11, a day symbolizing oneness, synchronicity, and alignment, we are reminded to bring forth that ideal, to bring forth that imagined nation, and to bring forth that dream of world peace and oneness and unity. Bring it forth and connect it with the power of spiritual practice, the power of meditation, the power of sangha with our collective and community practice, and with the power of mindful living throughout the day. When this happens, when we can combine the ideal with the power of this spiritual practice in community, then watch out world.

We Must Do It Together

The time of 'lone ranger' spirituality is no longer applicable. There were times in the past when it was wonderful, and different individuals could become enlightened by themselves and be on their own path. But today, in my opinion, we need a collective. We need to become enlightened together, so that there is enough power to transform and shift the collective global energy. I feel that we are at a point in time where we are heading towards global disaster. You see, we can no longer sustain our current lifestyles over time without completely ruining the planet's ecosystem and moving toward a global catastrophe.

However, I believe that within the next year, we have the opportunity to collectively shift the direction toward a global awakening, if we so choose. And so that is what this day is really about. It is not the end, and it is certainly not going to end a year from now either. It is an opportunity for a new beginning and to let go of the old ways, to let go of ways that have not worked. We have the opportunity now to practice and create a new beginning for ourselves and for the world.

So as we gather together, meditate together, dance together, sing together, and celebrate oneness together, let us reaffirm our dream of a world where there is love, peace, and harmony—a world where everyone feels cared for, nurtured, and supported on the path of enlightenment.

The secret has been with us all along. You see, the ideal and the power of practice in community is just Buddha, dharma, and sangha. In Christian language, it is the Christ ideal living out the Gospel truth in our daily lives, in the church, in the community, in the kingdom of heaven on earth. Whatever tradition you follow, it does not matter. All traditions point toward the same universal truths using different languages, different words, and different metaphors. But if you allow yourself to get caught up in only the symbols, instead of allowing them to draw you beyond the symbolism, then you are not allowing the truth to fully permeate your heart and life. You are stuck in forms, unable to see the essence. And that does not mean that forms are bad; forms are wonderful. I love forms, but forms are there to point us toward the direct experience of truth that is universal.

So use your Buddhist forms, your Christian forms, your Jewish forms, your Muslim forms, or whatever forms you enjoy. Use them to transform your communities and help the global awakening move beyond the forms to the essence of that truth. Follow the Buddha and the dharma and the sangha by awakening the ideal, the dream of true peace and enlightenment on the earth. And give it the power of dharma, of practice, of meditation, and of mindful living consistently, faithfully, and diligently. Do it in the collective energy of the sangha, of the community alongside your brothers and sisters on the path with you.

Alone We Are A Raindrop, Together We Are A River

As I have said before, we are all like little raindrops, beautiful, lovely, and cute little raindrops. But we evaporate very quickly by ourselves. And it is important to add our single raindrop to other raindrops so that together we will form a mighty river of enlightenment that cannot be stopped. That is what is required today on this date of 1-1, 1-1, 1-1; it is all about oneness. Yet there is more than just a single one because it takes all of our ones together to make the oneness. And that is what sangha really means. Each of us is a beautiful infinite one, but we must bring our individual ones together to create the true universal oneness. So add your one with the one next to you, and together we cannot be stopped: 1+1+1+1+1+1...

Let us just enjoy all of the energy that we collectively generate, and let us use that energy when we go home tonight, or when some of us stay for the 11:11 p.m. meditation. Use that energy when you go to sleep and when you wake up in the morning; continue flowing in this energy—let it flow; let it flow. Oneness of the whole world starts with you. Each of us needs to realize our oneness so that the whole world can realize its oneness.

But the whole world will not realize its oneness unless each of us realizes our own individual oneness. We are not one if there is a war inside—if your right brain is having a war with your left brain, if your head is having a war with your heart, or if your body is having a war with its spirit. We are all struggling with the war within, and that is why there is so much strife and turmoil in the world. Let us heal the inner disharmony within each of us and help create harmony amongst ourselves and throughout the whole world—that is the key.

So, do not think that you are not important. You are important! We need you. Do not sit back and think that other people will do the work. Do not tell yourself, "I am not really necessary." That is just not true; you are necessary. The very fact that you are alive at this time in history means a lot. It means you have a purpose, and maybe you have not remembered it yet, but you will. It may be today or it might be sometime in the next year, but you will remember it. And when you do, watch out world. Here we come!

Amitabha

Mindfulness, Monkey Mind, Sangha, and World Transformation

February 21, 2016-Dallas, Texas, Lunar New Year

Editor's Note: This was the last dharma talk given by Brother ChiSing before his passing on March 8, 2016.

While half of the practice of mindfulness is to get to a place of calm and peace, stillness and awareness, the other half is to just be with the noises, be with the body sensations, be with the thoughts, and accept them. Half of the practice is to be with the 'monkey mind' in this year of the monkey.

And if you do not realize that, then it is no wonder that you think you cannot meditate well. So part of meditation is to eventually come to a place of peace, stillness, non-stress, awareness, and acceptance—radical surrender and acceptance to what is. Because guess what? If you fight reality, reality wins every time. So let us not fight reality. Let us be with it, flow with it, and reality will dance with you and eventually transform you in the world.

Many centuries ago, St. Francis, a Bodhisattva from a different religious tradition told his monks to go out and preach the good news to every human and every creature and to use words only if necessary. You do not need to say a lot. People observe you—do they not? And they scrutinize you; that is why reality TV shows are so popular. They are looking for something different in you that maybe they can use for themselves. So if you become the dharma, then your attitude, your smile, your generosity, your awareness, your kindness, your way of walking, your way of talking, and your way of being in the world is already preaching the dharma. And you do not even have to say anything, unless necessary.

Just by our very existence, we exert a positive force around us wherever we are. Remember that the next time you gather together in sangha and meditation, you intensify the positive force. And remember that the next time you are in a waiting room or a hospital or anywhere, you are invisibly helping those in that place even just by simply being.

These words and this insight are not from a book. It comes from the dharma of my experience.

It's Our Presence, Not Words

I have been in the hospital so many times in the last two years. Sometimes I feel helpless and useless. And sometimes it is so hard to breathe nowadays that I cannot even do normal breath mindfulness meditation. I can't even do chanting meditation in the normal way. So I had to come up with creative new ways to practice. But you know, I realized in the hospital a couple of weeks ago that I am never useless. Just by my very existence, the existence as a human being, I already radiate the light invisibly. So the bottom line of our human existence is always positive light, no matter how many weird things you have done in your life—crazy things, poor choices. Just remember; the bottom line of who you are is always radiant, positive light. And that can never be erased—never, ever erased.

So if there is nothing else that you can do except just be there, remember that your very being is radiating and helping. So I was there in the hospital just being, not useless—no, just being and radiating. Perhaps someone else in the hospital near me needed my presence, whether they knew I was there or not. So if you find yourself in a place or situation that is not really pleasant, and you have no idea why you have to be there, just remember, perhaps the universe needs you to be there to add a little bit more light. It might have been too overwhelming in that moment for someone else without you. There is always more light when more than one of us is consciously in a place, consciously together in meditation and spiritual practices. *Wow!* Know that you have just added light, a radiant deposit of light in that place. You may not know everyone in the room, but you have affected everyone in the room with your presence. Do not forget that, please!

I have not been able to come to sangha for months because of my health, and I feel like it was not really good for me to come tonight, but I was so determined to come, no matter what, because I do not know when the next time will be that I can come. It is my deepest desire to be with the sangha every week. So think about that. If that is my deepest desire, can that be yours too? So many people make up excuses: "I'm too tired today to go to sangha" or "Oh, I don't need sangha," or "I can just meditate at home by myself." *No, please!* I want you to want sangha as much as I want sangha. I need sangha. I love sangha. And not only I, but everyone in this room needs me to be in sangha, and everyone in this room needs you to be in sangha for them.

I believe the ultimate destiny of humankind will be positive, that we will eventually overcome all these wars, discriminations and prejudices, fundamentalisms and persecutions, and all those nasty "monkey mind" habits. Sangha helps to make this possible. If you are not actively supporting your local sangha, this ultimate destiny will be slower paced, but it will still occur even though it may take a few more centuries. But for the sake of all suffering, that does not need to happen between now and then. I implore you to take refuge in the sangha and encourage others to take refuge in sangha.

So It Is Up To You

Will we have to go through all of this craziness for many more centuries? We all have free will. Will we choose to transform it all in one generation, in just 40 years? It is possible; I have seen it in visions. It is possible to completely transform this planet in just one generation, just 40 years. But I do not know if it is going to happen. I do not know if everyone is going to choose that, but it is possible. It is up to us.

So, definitely take refuge in Buddha, your enlightened nature. Definitely take refuge in the dharma, the teachings and practices and the radiance of being who you are. But most importantly, I think, take refuge and support the sangha, because that is where Buddha and dharma become real—as sangha.

Works by Brother ChiSing

BUDDHA Is My Refuge
New DHARMA Songs for the Contemporary SANGHA

Brother ChiSing's music CD! Contemporary Buddhist music (Spiritual Pop Music) inspired by the mindfulness teachings of Zen Master Thich Nhat Hanh offers positive music with a universal message. Brother ChiSing's music is available online at most music stores and streaming services or purchase directly at:

www.BrotherChiSing.com

108 REFLECTIONS
For The Daily Practice of Mindfulness and Meditation

This book will help you live life with more insight, more love, and more mindfulness. Brother ChiSing's brilliant mind, open heart, and childlike joy reveals the wonder of the Universe, ever available to each of us in the here and now. The depth of spiritual understanding and interfaith acceptance will make your soul sing with infinite light, infinite love, and infinite life. Brother ChiSing's book is available at online bookstores or directly at:

www.BrotherChiSing.com

Music by Cornell Kinderknecht, Co-Director, Awakening Heart, Dallas Meditation Center

DREAMTIME
Instrumental Music that Fills the Heart and Feeds the Soul

For nearly ten years, Cornell Kinderknecht's flute music, either performed live or via recording, was frequently a part of Brother ChiSing's workshops and meditation gatherings. Brother ChiSing often included Cornell's award-winning Dreamtime album in his course materials as a practice tool for mindfulness and meditation. Dreamtime transports you to a place where all things are possible—a place where you can be at peace while feeling energized, a place of mystique and wonder, and a place where you can play and let your imagination run free. Cornell Kinderknecht's music is available online at most music stores and streaming services or directly at:

www.cornellk.com

The Community

Awakening Heart
COMMUNITY OF MINDFUL LIVING

AWAKENING HEART (Community of Mindful Living)
Awakening Heart (Community of Mindful Living) is an interfaith mindfulness meditation practice community founded by Brother ChiSing and inspired by the practices and teachings of Zen Master Thich Nhat Hanh. Awakening Heart welcomes all people to participate in its weekly meditation gatherings, workshops, and classes located in the Dallas, Texas USA area. The community has multiple meditation practice groups: Awakening Heart Sangha, Wake Up Dallas—Young Enlightened Souls (YES), Interbeing Sangha, and Mindful Mondays—Practical Mindfulness for Everyday Living. Obtain additional information and listen to weekly talks at:
www.AwakeningHeart.org

DALLAS MEDITATION CENTER

Dallas Meditation Center is one of the first interfaith meditation centers in north Texas and is the home of Awakening Heart (Community of Mindful Living). It also hosts classes in yoga, tai chi, qigong and other genuine traditions of meditation and mindful living. The center routinely offers uplifting music concerts, celebratory spiritual events, and workshops on health and wellness. It is a gathering place to experience the JOY of mindful living. Obtain information on current activities or learn more about the Center at:

www.DallasMeditationCenter.com

ONE DHARMA AWAKENING HEART DALLAS MEDITATION CENTER

A US nonprofit 501(c)(3) human services and educational organization formed by Brother ChiSing. Through the work and programs of Awakening Heart and Dallas Meditation Center, the nonprofit organization provides meditation and life enrichment education to the community, helping individuals live a healthier and more mindful life. To find out more or to help support the organization, you may contact us through our website at:

www.DallasMeditationCenter.com

My Notes

www.ingramcontent.com/pod-product-compliance
Lightning Source LLC
Chambersburg PA
CBHW022104090426
42743CB00008B/716